AT TABLE
with FAMILY & FRIENDS

AT TABLE

with FAMILY *&* FRIENDS

HEARST BOOKS

NEW YORK

LIBRARY OF CONGRESS CATALOGING-IN-PUBLICATION DATA

Victoria at table with family and friends/
From the editors of Victoria magazine. -- 1st ed.
           p.   cm.
Includes index.
    ISBN   0-688-11662-0 (hardcover)
             1-58816-026-2 (paperback)
   I. Cookery. I. Victoria (New York, N.Y.)
   II. Title: At table with family and friends.
TX714.V53   1995
641.5--dc20   94-23779
                                CIP

Front cover photograph by Tom Eckerle

Back cover photographs by Steve Cohen (bottom left), Jeremy Samuelson (bottom
right), Michael Skott (top left), William Steele (top right)

Produced by Smallwood & Stewart, Inc., New York City

Designer: Susi Oberhelman

First Paperback Edition 2001

1 2 3 4 5 6 7 8 9 10

Printed in Singapore

www.victoriamag.com

CONTENTS

The Bountiful Table

Foreword

~

My grandmother was the best cook. Her apple pie is still legendary. And three generations of our family devotedly tout Aunt Mary's famous frosted creams. Sunday roasts, hearty fall suppers, holiday specialties ~ what an appetite I have for all these food memories.

The cooking was wonderful, but what is in my heart is the gathering of family and friends at table ~ dinner tables, picnic tables, breakfast tables ~ for truly that is what made our mealtimes the delights I remember. It still is. In this book, *Victoria* has collected that kind of spirit from all over America, from various parts of the world as well, in treasured recipes and creative cooking served with the attention to detail that makes us know that caring hands were at work for our pleasure and well being.

The French have a phrase, *cuisine de tendresse*. I learned on a May afternoon in a warm and loving home in Burgundy that there is no exact English translation, but there is a universal understanding. It is that when food is prepared and served with traditions of land and family, it is a wonderful gift. The cooking in this book is really the gift of many people, and the recipes are as dear to them as my grandmother's apple pie is to me. As your family and friends share this table with us at *Victoria*, we wish you good appetite and happy times.

NANCY LINDEMEYER

Founding Editor, Victoria Magazine

Notes About the Recipes

• All recipes call for large eggs. It is essential to use scrupulously clean beaters and bowls for beating egg whites so they will increase in volume and hold together. For easier handling and to keep your oven clean, we suggest placing pie tins, springform pans, and other pans that might overflow on a baking sheet to catch drips.

• To process jellies and pickles in a boiling-water bath, bring water to a boil in a large pot fitted with a wire rack. The water should be deep enough to cover the tops of the jars by an inch or two. Place the jars on the rack so they don't touch one another or the pot. Cover the pot and bring the water back to a boil. Boil as long as directed in the recipe. (Add one additional minute processing time for each 1,000 feet above sea level.) Cool the jars on a rack.

• When baking, ingredients should be at room temperature unless the recipe specifies otherwise. When cooking meat or fish, however, do not leave these raw ingredients on the counter for more than a short time. Thaw them in the refrigerator to prevent the possibility of harmful bacteria growing.

• We have used herbs and edible flowers in abundance throughout the book. Feel free to experiment with herbs you have on hand or in your garden if you don't have those specified in a recipe. While fresh herbs taste far better than dried, you can generally substitute dried in a one to three ratio. (For example, use one teaspoon of dried herbs in place of one tablespoon fresh.)

• When cooking or garnishing with flowers, be sure to use those grown without pesticides. Peppery nasturtiums can be found in some supermarkets, and the blossoms of everyday herbs, such as chives or thyme, are available at many farmers' markets. But they are just some of the many varieties that can add color and spark to food. Seek out growers who cultivate roses, stephanotis, Johnny-jump-ups, or marigolds for culinary uses.

The
Bountiful
Table

Fine Beginnings

This is food that cures, consoles, and speaks to our yearnings for a simpler way of life, when a pot of soup on the back burner imbued the kitchen, and perhaps the whole house, with the aroma of warmth and love. And a salad, shared with a special friend on a sunny afternoon, invited the kind of uncommon intimacy that we most desire.

COLD CUCUMBER BURNET SOUP

SERVES 6

½ cup (I stick) unsalted butter

I cup chopped onion

I medium-size cucumber, peeled, seeded, and chopped

¼ cup all-purpose flour

6 cups chicken stock

2 cups lightly packed chopped Boston lettuce

I cup chopped salad burnet leaves

½ cup chopped watercress

½ cup chopped chives

¼ cup chopped parsley

¾ cup heavy cream

Herb sprigs and thin cucumber slices, for garnish

Pesticide-free flowers, such as nasturtiums, borage, or chive blossoms, for garnish

1. In a heavy large pot, melt the butter over medium-low heat. Add the onion and cook, stirring often, until it is soft but not brown. Add the cucumber. Cook, stirring occasionally, for 5 minutes.

2. Stir in the flour. Cook, stirring constantly, for 5 minutes. In another pot, bring the stock to a boil. Gradually stir the stock into the onion mixture. Mix well and simmer for 15 minutes.

3. Stir in the lettuce, salad burnet, watercress, chives, and parsley. Simmer for 5 minutes.

4. Puree the soup in a blender or food processor in several batches. Pour it into a large bowl. Cover and refrigerate the soup until cold, at least 4 hours.

5. To serve, stir in the cream. Garnish the soup with fresh herbs, cucumber slices, and flowers.

GREEN-HERB SOUP

SERVES 2

1 cup chopped leaf lettuce

1 cup small watercress sprigs, chopped

3 scallions, minced (⅓ cup)

2 tablespoons chopped parsley or fresh chervil

1 tablespoon chopped fresh dill, or ¾ teaspoon dried dillweed

1 bay leaf

2½ cups chicken broth

1 tablespoon all-purpose flour

½ cup sour cream

Freshly ground pepper to taste

Pesticide-free dill sprigs and edible flowers, for garnish

1. In a medium-size saucepan, combine the lettuce, watercress, scallions, parsley, dill, the bay leaf, and the chicken broth.

2. Bring just to a boil. Reduce the heat to medium and simmer for 15 minutes, until the scallion is tender. Remove the pan from the heat.

3. In a small bowl, stir the flour into the sour cream until blended. Grad-ually whisk ½ cup hot broth into the sour cream. Slowly whisk the sour cream mixture into the soup.

4. Stir over medium-low heat for 3 minutes, until the soup is hot. Do not allow the soup to boil.

5. Remove the bay leaf. Season the soup with pepper. Garnish with dill sprigs and flowers.

WILD MUSHROOM BISQUE

SERVES 6 TO 8

3 tablespoons unsalted butter

12 ounces mixed wild mushrooms, sliced

3 tablespoons minced shallots

7¾ cups chicken stock

3 tablespoons uncooked long-grain rice

1 tablespoon tomato paste

1½ teaspoons fresh thyme, or ½ teaspoon dried

Black pepper to taste

¾ cup heavy cream

½ cup dry sherry

2 tablespoons finely minced red bell pepper

1. In a large skillet, melt the butter and sauté the mushrooms and shallots until tender. Using a slotted spoon, transfer the vegetables to a large soup pot, reserving the drippings in the skillet.

2. Add ¾ cup of the stock to the drippings. Bring the mixture to a boil, scraping up any browned bits from the bottom of the skillet. Reduce the heat. Cover and simmer for 5 minutes.

3. Pour the hot stock into the vegetables in the pot. Add the rice, tomato paste, thyme, and black pepper. Stir in the remaining 7 cups of stock. Bring the soup to a boil. Reduce the heat, cover, and simmer the soup for 1 hour.

4. Strain the soup, reserving both the vegetables and the stock. In a blender, puree the vegetables with some of the stock, in batches.

5. In the same pot, combine the pureed vegetables, any remaining stock, the cream, sherry, and red bell pepper. Heat gently, stirring occasionally, for 20 minutes. Do not allow the soup to boil.

CURRIED CARROT SOUP

SERVES 6 TO 8

You might find this soup on the menu at the Buffalo Springs Herb Farm in the Shenandoah Valley, where Don Haynie's extensive gardens supply the kitchen and provide the materials for wreaths and arrangements.

4 garlic cloves

4 tablespoons unsalted butter

1 pound carrots, chopped

3 celery stalks with tops, chopped

1 medium-size onion, chopped

1 medium-size potato, peeled and chopped

3 tablespoons all-purpose flour

2 tablespoons packed light brown sugar

1 cup milk

1 tablespoon chopped fresh rosemary, or 1 teaspoon dried

½ teaspoon curry powder

Salt and freshly ground pepper to taste

2 cups chicken stock

2 cups half-and-half

Dash of turmeric

2 tablespoons dry white wine

Chopped chives, for garnish

1. Preheat the oven to 325°F. Put the garlic cloves on a small pie plate and roast them for 30 minutes. Cool and peel them.

2. In a large saucepan, melt the butter and sauté the carrots, celery, onion, and potato over medium heat until tender, about 20 minutes.

3. Reduce the heat to low. Sprinkle the flour and brown sugar on the vegetables, tossing to coat. Stir in the milk until blended. Add the garlic, rosemary, and curry powder, and season with salt and pepper.

Mix well. Cook the soup over low heat, stirring often, for 15 minutes. Do not boil it.

4. Puree the soup in a blender in several batches, adding some of the stock to each batch.

5. Return the puree to the saucepan. Stir in the half-and-half and the turmeric. Cook over medium-low heat, stirring often, until it is heated through, about 15 minutes. Stir the wine into the soup. Garnish with fresh chives.

ROSEMARY

Long a symbol of remembrance, rosemary is an evergreen shrub with a robust flavor that calls to mind pine and spice. Rosemary leaves are used in lamb and chicken, bread, stuffings, and vinegar. Herb lovers can add a sprig to a decanted bottle of white wine, refrigerate it overnight, and serve it cold with hors d'oeuvres. Strong rosemary tea added to bath water makes for an invigorating experience.

CREAM OF ASPARAGUS SOUP

SERVES 4

An alternative, whimsical garnish to the one suggested below can be made with boiled, chilled beets. Cut a beet into thin slices, then cut out small hearts or stars to float on the surface of the soup.

1½ pounds asparagus

3 tablespoons unsalted butter

1 medium-size onion, thinly sliced

2 shallots, thinly sliced, plus 6 for garnish

¼ cup dry vermouth

4 cups vegetable or chicken stock

½ teaspoon salt (optional)

¼ teaspoon white pepper

¼ teaspoon ground nutmeg

1 cup heavy cream

⅓ cup all-purpose flour

4 chives, for garnish

1. Remove and discard the tough stems of the asparagus. Reserve 6 of the tips for garnish. Peel the asparagus if they are large. (Otherwise the outer layer may impart a bitterness to the soup.) Cut the asparagus in 1-inch lengths.

2. Melt the butter in a heavy large saucepan over medium heat. Cook the onion in the butter, stirring often, for 5 minutes. Add the shallots and cover with the vermouth. Cook until the onions are translucent, 5 minutes.

3. Add the stock and bring to a boil. Add the asparagus. Cover and cook the soup for 5 to 10 minutes, until the asparagus is very tender. Season the soup with the salt, white pepper, and nutmeg.

4. Allow the soup to cool slightly. Strain the soup and reserve the liquid in the saucepan.

5. Puree the vegetables in a blender or food processor and return the puree to the liquid in the saucepan.

Strain the soup through a fine sieve to remove any asparagus fiber. Return the soup to the saucepan.

6. In a medium-size bowl, gradually whisk the cream into the flour until the flour dissolves. Slowly whisk that mixture into the soup. Whisk the soup over moderately high heat until it is thickened and boiling.

7. For the garnish, blanch the 6 reserved asparagus tips in boiling salted water for about 4 minutes. Drain. Cut each tip in half lengthwise. Blanch the chives for 1 minute, or until wilted. Remove them from the water and pat them dry on paper towels.

8. For each serving, tie 3 asparagus pieces into a bundle using a chive. Peel and halve the shallots lengthwise. Blanch them for about 5 minutes. Drain. Arrange 3 shallot halves on top of each serving of soup. Place an asparagus bundle on top of each shallot cluster.

VEGETABLES AS SERVING DISHES

*A*corn or butternut
squashes make
earthy, appealing serving
dishes. Peppers
and oranges work well, too.
Cut them and hollow
them out carefully so they
will be leakproof.

CREAM OF YELLOW PEPPER SOUP

SERVES 4 TO 6

*T*his soup is equally delicious and colorful made with red bell peppers. Or prepare one batch with yellow bell peppers and one with red, then serve them together in shallow bowls in "yin-yang" fashion, so that each serving is half yellow, half red ~ the presentation will be gorgeous.

2 tablespoons olive oil

I medium-size onion, sliced

3 medium-size yellow bell peppers, thinly sliced

I garlic clove, finely chopped

½ cup dry white wine

½ teaspoon salt

¼ teaspoon cayenne

4 cups vegetable stock or chicken broth

I cup heavy cream

¼ cup all-purpose flour

Sour cream and bay sprigs, or thyme, marjoram, or oregano leaves, for garnish

I. Heat the olive oil in a large heavy saucepan. Add the onion and cook over medium heat until it begins to soften, about 5 minutes.

2. Set aside a quarter of I pepper for garnish. Add the remaining yellow peppers and the garlic to the onions. Continue to cook for 5 minutes, stirring occasionally.

3. Add the white wine and cook over moderately high heat for about 5 minutes, until the wine has been reduced so that it just moistens the bottom of the pan. Sprinkle with the salt and cayenne.

4. Stir in the stock. Bring the mixture to a boil, reduce the heat, and cover. Simmer over medium heat, stirring occasionally, for 10 to 12 minutes, until the vegetables are soft.

5. Allow the soup to cool slightly.

6. Strain the soup, reserving the liquid in the saucepan. Puree the vegetables in a blender or in the bowl of a food processor. Return the puree to the saucepan.

7. In a medium-size bowl, gradually whisk the heavy cream into the flour. Slowly whisk that mixture into the soup. Whisk the soup over moderately high heat until it is thickened and boiling.

8. Pour the soup into a tureen or into individual serving bowls. To garnish, pipe the sour cream through a pastry tube or from a squeeze bottle in a decorative pattern over the soup. Garnish the soup with fresh herbs and julienne strips of the reserved pepper.

Salmon & Wild Mushroom Chowder

SERVES 4

This hearty chowder has warmed many a soul and body at River Wildlife, a lodge in the Wisconsin wilderness where Aina Henegar is known for her "country gourmet" food.

PEPPER CROUTONS

2 large slices sourdough bread, crusts removed

2 tablespoons unsalted butter

I teaspoon cracked pepper

¼ teaspoon salt

SALMON CHOWDER

⅓ cup unsalted butter

⅓ cup all-purpose flour

2 cups chicken broth

I cup clam juice

I large potato, peeled and chopped

⅓ cup dry white wine

2 teaspoons lemon juice

1⅓ cups flaked poached salmon, bones and skin removed

I cup chopped wild mushrooms, preferably shiitake

⅓ cup chopped carrot

⅓ cup chopped celery

⅓ cup chopped onion

⅓ cup chopped green bell pepper

⅓ cup chopped red bell pepper

⅓ cup chopped yellow bell pepper

½ teaspoon Worcestershire sauce

¼ teaspoon celery seed

¼ teaspoon black pepper

¼ teaspoon seasoned salt

⅛ teaspoon minced garlic

⅛ teaspoon bottled hot pepper sauce

⅔ cup heavy cream

⅔ cup half-and-half

I. To make the croutons, cut the bread in ½-inch cubes. Melt 2 tablespoons butter in a medium-size skillet over medium-high heat. Add the bread cubes, I teaspoon pepper, and ¼ teaspoon salt. Cook, tossing constantly, until the bread cubes are toasted. Set aside.

2. To make the chowder, melt ⅓ cup butter in a small saucepan, over medium heat. Stir in the flour until smooth. Cook, stirring constantly, for 2 minutes. Set aside.

3. In a large saucepan, combine the chicken broth, clam juice, and potato. Bring to a boil. Reduce the heat, cover, and simmer for 10 minutes.

4. Stir in the wine, lemon juice, salmon, mushrooms, carrot, celery, onion, all the peppers, the Worcestershire sauce, celery seed, black pepper, seasoned salt, garlic, and hot pepper sauce. Bring to a boil. Reduce the heat, cover, and simmer for 15 to 20 minutes, until the vegetables are tender.

5. Gradually stir in the heavy cream, half-and-half, and the flour mixture. Cook the chowder, stirring constantly, over medium heat until the mixture thickens and boils.

6. Ladle the chowder into bowls or cups. Top with croutons.

BAKED ONION SOUP

SERVES 6 TO 8

Many homemakers in Victorian times looked to Isabella Beeton for advice on cooking and on running their households. Recently, London chef Antony Worrall-Thompson included this soup, generously laced with Madeira, in a menu Mrs. Beeton might have devised for Christmas dinner. But don't leave it for special occasions; it is warming and welcome on any cold day.

7 cups chicken broth

2 thyme sprigs

2 bay leaves

6 tablespoons unsalted butter

2 tablespoons vegetable oil

3 garlic cloves, finely chopped

3 pounds white onions, thinly sliced

¾ teaspoon sugar

¾ teaspoon salt

¾ teaspoon freshly ground black pepper

⅓ cup all-purpose flour

1½ cups dry white wine

¼ cup Madeira

1¾ cups grated Gruyère

6 to 8 slices French bread, cut 1 inch thick and toasted

1. In a large saucepan, bring the chicken broth, thyme sprigs, and bay leaves to a boil. Remove from the heat. Cover and let stand.

2. In a heavy large pot, heat the butter and oil over medium heat. Add the garlic and onions. Cook for 45 to 55 minutes, stirring often, until the onions turn light golden brown.

3. Sprinkle the sugar, salt, pepper, and flour over the onions. Stir until well blended. Cook, stirring constantly, for 5 minutes.

4. Pour in the white wine, stirring to scrape up any browned bits from the bottom of the pot. Stir in the hot stock. Bring the soup to a boil. Reduce the heat and simmer for 30 minutes, stirring occasionally.

5. Remove the bay leaves and thyme sprigs. Stir in the Madeira.

6. Preheat the oven to 350°F.

7. Sprinkle a little grated Gruyère in the bottom of 6 to 8 ovenproof 20-ounce soup bowls. Arrange the bowls on a baking sheet.

8. Pour hot soup into the bowls. Top each serving with a slice of French bread and the remaining grated Gruyère. Bake for 8 to 10 minutes, until the cheese is golden.

MESCLUN AU CHÈVRE

SERVES 4

1 teaspoon herbes de Provence

1 teaspoon Dijon mustard

1 garlic clove, minced

¼ teaspoon salt

¼ teaspoon coarsely cracked black pepper

2 tablespoons white wine vinegar

¼ cup extra virgin olive oil

6 cups mesclun or a variety of baby lettuces

4 ounces aged chèvre, such as Tomme de Chèvre

1. In a screw-top jar, combine the herbes de Provence, Dijon mustard, garlic, salt, pepper, wine vinegar, and olive oil. Cover and shake to blend.

2. In a salad bowl, toss the mesclun with the vinaigrette. Arrange the mesclun on 4 chilled salad plates. Using a vegetable peeler, shave the chèvre in a pattern on each salad. If the cheese is not firm enough to shave, crumble it on each salad.

ZESTY PEA SALAD

SERVES 6

2 cups fresh or frozen peas

1 cup fresh sugar snap or snow peas

½ cup sour cream

2 tablespoons chopped chives

2 tablespoons chopped cilantro

2 tablespoons chopped mint

1 tablespoon white wine vinegar

1 teaspoon curry powder

Salt and freshly ground pepper to taste

Leaf lettuce, for garnish

Herb sprigs, for garnish

1. Blanch the fresh peas in boiling water for 2 or 3 minutes, or run hot water over the frozen peas until they thaw. Drain and cool.

2. In a large bowl, combine the peas and sugar snap peas.

3. To make the dressing, combine the sour cream, chives, cilantro, mint, wine vinegar, curry powder, and salt and pepper in a small bowl. Using a fork or whisk, mix well.

4. Fold the dressing into the peas. Spoon the salad into a lettuce-lined bowl. Garnish with herb sprigs.

ENDIVE & WATERCRESS SALAD

SERVES 4

The five-star Inn at Little Washington, tucked into the Blue Ridge Mountains of Virginia, spares no romantic detail. Chef and co-owner Patrick O'Connell seeks ~ and finds ~ "a happy marriage of peasant and grand cuisine."

4 ounces soft chèvre, preferably Virginia or Montrachet

1 teaspoon finely minced dill

1 teaspoon finely minced parsley

1 teaspoon finely minced rosemary

1 teaspoon finely minced tarragon

¼ cup olive oil

2 tablespoons walnut oil

2 tablespoons white wine vinegar

½ teaspoon balsamic vinegar

1 tablespoon finely chopped shallots

1 small garlic clove, minced

¼ teaspoon dry mustard

Salt and white pepper to taste

1 bunch watercress

4 poached or canned pear halves

2 (4-ounce) heads Belgian endive

Croutons, crumbled bacon, and toasted walnuts, for garnish

1. Roll the chèvre between two sheets of waxed paper until it is ¼ inch thick. (If the chèvre is too firm to roll out, cut it in ¼-inch slices, then cut heart shapes from the slices.) With heart-shaped cookie cutters, cut out four 2-inch hearts and four 1-inch hearts.

2. Combine the dill, parsley, rosemary, and tarragon on a piece of waxed paper. Press the tops of the hearts in the herbs to coat.

3. In a screw-top jar, combine the olive oil, walnut oil, wine vinegar, balsamic vinegar, shallots, garlic, dry mustard, and salt and pepper. Cover and shake until blended.

4. Arrange a mound of watercress in the center of each of 4 serving plates. Cut each pear half in 5 slices. Alternate 5 endive leaves and 5 pear slices spoke-fashion around the watercress.

5. Shake the vinaigrette; drizzle it over the salads. Garnish each salad with a large and a small chèvre heart and croutons, crumbled bacon, and walnuts.

*Most fresh herbs will
keep for a week in the
refrigerator. Those with tender
stems, such as parsley,
should be set in a glass of
water and covered
with a plastic bag. Woody-
stemmed herbs, thyme
and rosemary among them,
should be sealed in a bag.*

*For longer storage,
tender-stemmed herbs can be
pureed and preserved
in oil or water. Use about
half a cup of liquid
for two cups of herbs.
Freeze the mixture.*

Herb Salad

SERVES 6

1 medium-size cucumber

1 large head leaf lettuce

2 to 4 tablespoons lightly
packed chopped chives,
sorrel, or parsley

¼ cup lightly packed chopped
basil, lovage, or marjoram

3 tablespoons walnut or
hazelnut oil

2 tablespoons vegetable oil

4 teaspoons cider vinegar

Pinch of salt

⅔ cup pine nuts

Pesticide-free edible flowers,
for garnish

1. Peel 5 strips from the cucumber, leaving thin strips of peel in between. Cut the cucumber in thin slices. Cover and refrigerate.
2. Tear the lettuce into a salad bowl. Add the herbs. Cover and refrigerate until ready to serve.

3. Combine the oils, vinegar, and salt in a screw-top jar. Cover and shake well to blend the dressing.
4. To serve, add the cucumbers and pine nuts to the greens. Drizzle with dressing and toss to coat. Garnish the salad with the flowers.

Sorrel & Nectarine Salad

SERVES 6

3 tablespoons raspberry
vinegar

1 teaspoon Dijon mustard

5 tablespoons olive
or vegetable oil

Pinch of sugar

Salt and pepper to taste

⅓ cup walnut halves

4 cups torn butter lettuce or
other mixed greens

1½ cups sorrel leaves, cut
lengthwise in strips

2 or 3 ripe nectarines, pitted
and sliced

1. In a screw-top jar, combine the vinegar, mustard, oil, sugar, and salt and pepper. Cover and shake vigorously until the dressing is blended.
2. Preheat the oven to 300°F. Spread the walnuts in a pie plate. Toast the walnuts for 5 to 8 minutes;

be careful that they do not burn.
3. Put the lettuce, sorrel, and nectarines in a chilled salad bowl. Shake the dressing. Pour it over the salad. Sprinkle with the walnuts and toss gently. Serve the salad on chilled plates.

Tomato-Mushroom Salad

2 pints cherry tomatoes
1 pound small mushrooms
1 medium-size red onion,
  finely chopped (1 cup)
2 tablespoons chopped chives
2 garlic cloves, minced

1 teaspoon sugar
½ teaspoon salt
2 tablespoons vegetable oil
1 tablespoon white wine
  vinegar

1. In a bowl, combine the tomatoes, mushrooms, and red onion.
2. In a small bowl, mix well the chives, garlic, sugar, and salt. Stir in the oil and vinegar until blended. Pour the dressing over the vegetables and toss to coat. Cover and refrigerate for several hours before serving.

New Potato Salad with Hazelnuts

2 tablespoons red wine vinegar
¼ teaspoon Dijon mustard
½ teaspoon salt
Freshly ground pepper to taste
¼ cup olive oil
2 tablespoons hazelnut oil

2 pounds small new red
  potatoes
1 cup hazelnuts
2 tablespoons chopped chives
2 tablespoons chopped parsley

1. In a small bowl, combine the vinegar, mustard, salt, and pepper. Whisk until blended. Gradually whisk in the olive and hazelnut oils in a thin stream until blended.
2. Preheat the oven to 350°F.
3. Scrub but do not peel the potatoes. Steam them until tender, 15 to 25 minutes. Cool.
4. While the potatoes are cooling, spread the hazelnuts on a baking sheet. Toast them in the preheated oven for 10 minutes. Rub the hot nuts in a tea towel to remove their skins. Chop the hazelnuts coarsely.
5. When they are cool enough to handle, cut the potatoes into small pieces. In a large bowl, combine them with the nuts, chives, and parsley. Whisk the vinaigrette and drizzle it over the salad. Toss gently. Serve the potato salad warm or at room temperature.

From the Sideboard

The marvelous flavor of homegrown vegetables was no stranger to our grandparents, but for a while technology seemed to rob us of a bit of that wonder. The tide is turning again, with farmers' markets growing and new choices turning up at supermarkets. Vegetables are taking center stage, and some of these dishes are as satisfying on their own as they are when they accompany meat and fish dishes.

Carrot & Parsnip Bunches

MAKES 5 OR 6 BUNCHES

1 bunch long scallion tops
  or chives

4 medium-size carrots

4 medium-size parsnips

½ teaspoon dried marjoram

½ teaspoon dried chervil

½ teaspoon dried basil

½ teaspoon dried tarragon

1 tablespoon unsalted butter,
  melted

1. Pour hot water to a depth of ½ inch in a large saucepan. Place a steamer basket in the saucepan. Spread the scallion tops in the basket. Bring the water to a boil over high heat, then reduce the heat to medium. Cover and steam for 1 minute. Plunge the scallion tops in ice water to stop the cooking.

2. Peel and cut the carrots and parsnips into pencil-size sticks about 4 inches long. Gather the carrot and parsnip sticks into 5 or 6 bunches of 5 sticks each and tie each bunch together with a scallion top.

3. Place the bunches in the same steamer. Mix all the herbs together, and sprinkle them over the carrots and parsnips. Bring to a boil over high heat, then reduce the heat to medium. Cover and steam the vegetables for about 10 minutes, until crisp-tender.

4. Gently lift the bunches onto a serving platter. Drizzle with the melted butter.

CHILLED SPRING VEGETABLES

SERVES 4

This imaginative presentation for vegetables in a vinaigrette comes from Frank Brough, chef at Victoria & Albert's, an elegant restaurant at Disney World in Florida. His meals are based on fresh seasonal ingredients, including the harvest from the hotel's own herb garden.

CARROT & GINGER VINAIGRETTE

½ cup white vinegar

2 tablespoons chopped gingerroot

½ cup fresh carrot juice

¼ cup orange juice

I teaspoon minced shallots

¼ teaspoon minced garlic

I cup vegetable oil (preferably grapeseed)

Salt and pepper to taste

CHILLED SPRING VEGETABLES

4 fresh baby artichokes or 8 frozen artichoke hearts, cooked and drained

Lemon juice

24 fresh green beans

16 stalks white or green asparagus

4 small carrots

I leek top, cut in 4 ribbons

4 kumquats

4 small heads baby red-tipped leaf lettuce

4 golden chanterelle or other wild mushrooms

4 baby zucchini, halved lengthwise

4 baby yellow summer squash, halved lengthwise

Seasoned cooking oil

8 red plum tomatoes, halved lengthwise

4 yellow plum tomatoes, halved lengthwise

Thyme or other herb sprigs, for garnish

I. To make the vinaigrette, bring the vinegar and gingerroot to a boil in a small saucepan. Cool to room temperature and strain, measuring ⅓ cup of vinegar.
2. In a blender, combine the ginger vinegar, carrot juice, orange juice, shallots, and garlic. With the blender running, slowly drizzle in the oil. Season with salt and pepper, and cover.
3. Remove the outer leaves from the baby artichokes. Snip off the prickly ends from the tips of the remaining

leaves. Brush the cut surfaces with lemon juice to prevent discoloring.

4. To make the vegetables, blanch separately the green beans, asparagus, carrots, leek ribbons, and artichokes in a large nonreactive pot of salted boiling water. Cool each quickly in ice water and drain. Quarter the artichokes and remove the fuzzy choke from the center.

5. Slice off both ends of the kumquats. Hollow each with an apple corer, creating a vase. Stuff lettuce leaves into each kumquat vase. Tie the green beans into 4 bundles with leek ribbons.

6. Brush the chanterelles, zucchini, and squash with seasoned oil. Grill or broil them 4 inches from the heat until tender, turning once. Cool them to room temperature.

7. Whisk the vinaigrette and pour some on each of 4 serving plates. Arrange the asparagus and carrots, artichokes, kumquat vases, green beans, red and yellow tomatoes, chanterelles, zucchini, and squash on the plates. Garnish with herb sprigs.

Early Plantation Sugar Snap Peas & Baby Onions

SERVES 8

This recipe was part of a menu for a luncheon in Washington, D.C., in honor of Queen Elizabeth's 1991 visit. To plan the menu, caterer Deborah Allen read the cookbooks of Martha Washington and of Thomas Jefferson, who grew thirty varieties of peas at Monticello.

I pound pearl onions, peeled

I tablespoon unsalted butter

I pound fresh sugar snap peas

¼ cup toasted pine nuts, for garnish

1. In a large pot of salted boiling water, blanch the onions for 12 to 14 minutes until tender. Remove them with a slotted spoon and toss them with ½ tablespoon of the butter. Cover to keep warm.

2. In the same pot, blanch the peas for 2 minutes until crisp-tender. Remove them with a slotted spoon and toss with the remaining butter.

3. Mix the onions and peas together. Garnish the vegetables with the toasted pine nuts.

MAPLED BRUSSELS SPROUTS

SERVES 6 TO 8

4 tablespoons unsalted butter

¼ cup pure maple syrup

2 tablespoons honey mustard

½ teaspoon prepared
horseradish

Freshly ground pepper

2 pounds (8 cups) fresh
Brussels sprouts

1. In a small saucepan, melt the butter over medium-low heat. Add the maple syrup, mustard, horseradish, and pepper. Whisk until smooth. Cook, stirring occasionally, for about 5 minutes. Remove from the heat.

2. Halve any large Brussels sprouts. Steam the sprouts until tender but still firm, about 12 to 15 minutes.

3. Pour the hot maple sauce over hot Brussels sprouts, and toss gently to mix.

GRILLED VEGETABLE PLATTER

SERVES 4

This version of grilled vegetables was conceived by Gary Crouse, chef at Caffe Cielo in New York City. To roast peppers, place them on a baking sheet and broil them 3 to 4 inches from the heat. Use tongs to turn them often, until they are blistered on all sides, about 20 minutes; don't worry if parts of the skin blacken. Place the peppers in a paper bag for 10 minutes to steam. Then peel and cut them as desired.

Coarse salt

1 medium-size eggplant, sliced
lengthwise

1 medium-size zucchini, sliced
lengthwise

1 Belgian endive, quartered

1 small head radicchio

Extra virgin olive oil

1 red bell pepper, roasted,
peeled, quartered
lengthwise, and seeded

1 yellow bell pepper,
roasted, peeled, quartered
lengthwise, and seeded

1 green bell pepper,
roasted, peeled, quartered
lengthwise, and seeded

2 tablespoons Gorgonzola

1. Preheat the oven to 450°F.

2. Sprinkle a griddle with coarse salt and heat it. Brown the eggplant and zucchini lightly on the griddle, turning often. Drain on paper towels.

3. Brush the endive and radicchio with olive oil. Grill until golden brown. Drain on paper towels.

4. Arrange all the vegetables on an ovenproof platter. Bake for 5 minutes.

5. Sprinkle the vegetables with the Gorgonzola and bake 1 minute longer, or until the cheese melts.

6. Use a paper towel to remove excess liquid from the platter. Sprinkle the vegetables with 1 tablespoon of olive oil and serve them hot.

Onion Tart with Spinach & Pine Nuts

SERVES 6

Charlotte's Piecrust
   (page 188)

3 tablespoons unsalted butter

½ pound onions, thinly sliced

½ pound spinach, stems removed and leaves coarsely chopped (6 cups)

4 eggs

1½ cups half-and-half

1 teaspoon salt

¼ teaspoon pepper

¼ teaspoon freshly grated nutmeg

2 tablespoons toasted pine nuts

2 tablespoons grated Parmesan

1. Preheat the oven to 400°F.

2. Line a 10-inch tart pan with the pastry dough. Prick the pastry with a fork every half inch. Line the pastry with a double thickness of foil and fill the foil with dried beans. Bake the tart on a baking sheet for 10 minutes. Remove the beans and foil. Continue baking the shell until golden, 5 to 10 minutes more. Cool the shell on a rack.

3. Reduce the heat to 350°F.

4. Melt the butter in a large skillet. Cook the onion in the butter over medium heat for 12 to 15 minutes, until transparent, stirring often. Remove the pan from the heat and stir in the spinach until it is wilted.

5. In a medium-size bowl, whisk the eggs, half-and-half, salt, pepper, and grated nutmeg.

6. Spoon the onion and spinach mixture evenly into the pastry shell. Pour the egg mixture on top. Sprinkle the surface with the pine nuts and grated Parmesan.

7. Bake the tart on a baking sheet for 35 to 40 minutes, until a cake tester inserted in the center comes out clean. Let the tart stand for 10 minutes before serving.

VEGETABLE TART

SERVES 8 TO 10

PASTRY

1½ cups all-purpose flour

¼ teaspoon salt

½ cup (1 stick) cold unsalted butter, cut in 8 pieces

2 tablespoons cold unsalted margarine, cut in 2 pieces

1 egg

ZUCCHINI FILLING

2 tablespoons olive oil

3 small zucchini, sliced (3 cups)

½ teaspoon dried basil

½ teaspoon dried oregano

¼ teaspoon salt

Freshly ground pepper to taste

ONION FILLING

1 to 2 tablespoons olive oil

2 large onions, chopped (3 cups)

1 teaspoon dried thyme

¼ teaspoon salt

Freshly ground pepper to taste

1 tablespoon all-purpose flour

1 egg

SPINACH TOPPING

1 (10-ounce) package frozen chopped spinach, thawed and squeezed dry

1 cup shredded Swiss cheese

¼ teaspoon salt

Freshly ground nutmeg to taste

Freshly ground pepper to taste

1. To make the pastry, place the 1½ cups flour, ¼ teaspoon salt, the butter, and the margarine in the bowl of a food processor. Process 8 to 10 times with on/off turns, until the mixture resembles peas. Add the egg. With the processor running, add 2 tablespoons of very cold water. Process just until the dough comes together.

2. Shape the dough into a disk, wrap, and chill it for 2 hours.

3. On a floured board, roll the pastry to fit into an 11-inch tart pan. Prick the bottom and side of the pastry. Chill for 20 to 30 minutes.

4. Preheat the oven to 375°F. Cover the pastry with foil and fill with dried beans. Bake the tart on a baking sheet for 10 minutes.

5. Remove the beans and foil. Prick the crust again, bake for 10 minutes, and let cool.

6. To make the zucchini filling, heat 2 tablespoons olive oil in a large skillet. Sauté the zucchini with the basil, oregano, ¼ teaspoon salt, and the pepper for 3 to 4 minutes, stirring often. Remove the vegetables from the skillet with a slotted spoon.

7. To make the onion filling, add 1 to 2 tablespoons olive oil to the same skillet, if necessary. Sauté the onions with the thyme, ¼ teaspoon salt, and the pepper for 8 to 10 minutes, or until soft, stirring often.

8. Reduce the heat. Stir in 1 tablespoon flour and cook for 2 minutes. Remove from the heat.

9. With a fork, beat the egg in a medium-size bowl. Add the onions and mix well.

10. To make the spinach topping, toss the spinach with the Swiss cheese, ¼ teaspoon salt, nutmeg, and pepper.

11. Arrange the zucchini slices to cover the bottom of the pastry. Sprinkle the spinach mixture on top. Spread the onion mixture on top of the spinach.

12. Bake the tart on a baking sheet for 35 to 40 minutes. Cool the tart 5 minutes before cutting.

CHINA MARKINGS

The rule of thumb for reading the marks on the underside of china is simple. If there is no mark, the piece was made before 1891, when the United States government began requiring imported china to indicate its country of origin. Pieces labeled only by country probably were made from 1891 to 1914. Thereafter, all imported china was marked "Made in . . .," specifying the country.

Vegetable Flans

SERVES 6

I pound broccoli or carrots,
   cooked and drained
¼ cup unsalted butter
3 eggs
½ cup milk

½ cup heavy cream
½ teaspoon salt
½ teaspoon ground nutmeg
⅛ teaspoon pepper

1. Preheat the oven to 375°F. Butter six 6-ounce custard cups generously.
2. In the bowl of a food processor, puree the vegetable and butter. Add the eggs, milk, cream, salt, nutmeg, and pepper. Process until smooth.
3. Set the custard cups in a baking pan. Pour hot water to a depth of I inch around the cups. Spoon about ⅔ cup of the vegetable mixture into each prepared custard cup.
4. Bake for 40 to 45 minutes, until the flans are firm and a knife inserted off-center comes out clean. Let the flans stand for 10 minutes on a wire rack.
5. Loosen the edges with a knife and invert the flans onto serving plates. To serve the flans at a later time, invert the cups into an empty baking pan. Cover the flans and refrigerate them. Reheat them, covered, in a 375°F. oven for 20 to 25 minutes, until heated through.

Celeriac & Potato Bake

SERVES 6 TO 8

I teaspoon salt
2 tablespoons lemon juice
I (I-pound) celeriac
4 large potatoes
3 eggs
I cup light cream

I cup milk
I large garlic clove, crushed
¾ cup grated Gruyère
Salt and pepper to taste

1. Bring a large pot of water to a boil. Add the salt and I tablespoon of the lemon juice.
2. While the water is heating, peel the celeriac. Immediately place it in a bowl of cold water with the remaining tablespoon of lemon juice to prevent darkening.
3. Peel and quarter the potatoes. Cut the celeriac in eighths. Drop the vegetables into the boiling water. Return to a boil and cook for 13 to 15 minutes, until almost tender. Drain the vegetables and cool in cold water. Dry on paper towels. Cut the vegetables into thin slices.

4. Preheat the oven to 350°F. Butter a 10 by 6 by 1½-inch baking dish.
5. In a medium-size bowl, whisk together the eggs, cream, and milk.
6. Layer half the celeriac and potatoes with half the garlic and one third of the Gruyère, and season with salt and pepper. Pour half the egg mixture over the vegetables.

Repeat the layers. Sprinkle the vegetables with the remaining cheese. (The dish will be very full.) Set the dish on a baking sheet.
7. Bake the vegetables for 1¼ hours, until the casserole is set in the center. Let the casserole stand for 10 minutes before serving.

GRATIN DAUPHINOIS

SERVES 6 TO 8

The French word *gratin* is used to describe a vegetable baked with a cheese sauce, as well as the dish in which it is baked. Here, the humble potato, combined with some classic ingredients~garlic, cream, and cheese~takes on a sophisticated air.

3 garlic cloves, finely chopped

2½ cups heavy cream

2 pounds baking potatoes, peeled and thinly sliced (5 cups)

2 shallots, finely chopped

Salt and freshly ground white pepper to taste

Freshly ground nutmeg to taste

2 teaspoons dried thyme

2 eggs, beaten

1¾ cups grated Parmesan and Gruyère mixed together

4 tablespoons unsalted butter

1. Preheat the oven to 350°F. Generously butter a 12 by 7½ by 2-inch baking dish. Sprinkle with chopped garlic to coat the bottom and sides.
2. In a medium-size saucepan, bring the cream to a boil. Remove from the heat and cover to keep warm.
3. Pat the potato slices dry on paper towels. In a large bowl, toss the potatoes with the shallots, salt, pepper, nutmeg, and thyme. Add the eggs and ½ cup of the cheese. Mix well.

Arrange even layers of the potato mixture in the prepared baking dish.
4. Pour the warm cream over the potatoes. Sprinkle with the remaining cheese and dot with the butter. Cover the dish with buttered foil and place on a baking sheet.
5. Bake for 45 minutes. Remove the foil and bake for 30 to 45 minutes more, until the potatoes are tender throughout. Let stand for 10 minutes before serving.

BASIL

Basil's heady aroma and pungent flavor are grace notes for dishes of many cuisines, from sauces and soups to salads and vegetables. Varieties include a citrusy lemon basil and a strong-scented opal basil. Although perishable, basil will keep a few days in the refrigerator if stood upright in a glass of water. Cover the leaves with a damp paper towel and then loosely with a plastic bag.

HERB-ROASTED NEW POTATOES

SERVES 6 TO 8

3 pounds small new potatoes, preferably Red Bliss (about 42 potatoes)

½ cup olive oil

I tablespoon chopped fresh rosemary, or I teaspoon dried

I tablespoon chopped fresh thyme, or I teaspoon dried

I tablespoon chopped parsley

Salt and pepper to taste

1. Preheat the oven to 375°F. Dip each potato in a measuring cup holding the oil, turning to coat evenly, then arrange the potatoes in a single layer in a 13 by 9 by 2-inch baking dish. Drizzle any remaining oil over the potatoes.

2. Sprinkle the potatoes with the rosemary, thyme, and parsley, and season with salt and pepper. Toss to mix.

3. Bake for 35 to 55 minutes, depending on the size of the potatoes, until tender. Turn the potatoes over occasionally during cooking.

LEMON BASIL HERBED RICE

SERVES 4 TO 6

2 tablespoons unsalted butter

3 tablespoons finely chopped onion

I cup uncooked long-grain rice

¼ cup chopped lemon basil

I small bay leaf

I tablespoon chopped parsley

Several drops bottled hot pepper sauce

2½ cups chicken stock

Salt and pepper to taste

1. Preheat the oven to 400°F.

2. Melt the butter in an ovenproof medium-size saucepan over medium heat and cook the onion, stirring often, for about 5 minutes, until translucent. Add the rice. Cook, stirring constantly, for 3 minutes.

3. Stir in the lemon basil, bay leaf, parsley, hot pepper sauce, and stock. Bring to a boil. Cover tightly.

4. Bake for 20 to 25 minutes, until the rice is tender. Season with salt and pepper. Fluff the rice with a fork and remove the bay leaf.

Confetti Rice with Two Basils

SERVES 6

2 scallions, finely chopped

3 tablespoons finely chopped green basil

¼ cup lemon juice

⅓ cup plus ½ teaspoon olive oil

Salt to taste

¼ teaspoon pepper, plus additional to taste

I cup uncooked rice

2 large ears fresh corn, or I (10-ounce) package frozen whole-kernel corn, cooked and drained

I small red pimiento, finely chopped

½ cup finely chopped celery or fennel bulb

¼ cup chopped purple opal basil

2 tablespoons chopped parsley

I. In a screw-top jar, combine the scallions, green basil, lemon juice, olive oil, salt, and ¼ teaspoon pepper. Cover and shake well.
2. Cook the rice in salted water according to package directions just until tender. At the same time, cook the corn on the cob in salted boiling water for 6 to 8 minutes, until tender. Cut the kernels off the cobs.
3. In a bowl, combine the hot rice and the corn. Shake the dressing and pour over the rice, tossing to coat. Cool to room temperature.
4. Toss in the pimiento, celery, purple basil, and parsley. Season with salt and pepper. Serve at room temperature.

Barley & Wild Rice Pilaf

SERVES 8

I (6-ounce) package long-cooking long-grain-and-wild-rice mix (reserve seasoning mix)

I cup quick-cooking barley

½ cup (I stick) unsalted butter

½ cup finely chopped red onion

I teaspoon dried thyme

½ teaspoon pepper

¼ teaspoon ground rosemary

I quart beef stock

I. Preheat the oven to 375°F.
2. In a large skillet, brown the rice and barley in the butter for about 10 minutes, stirring often.
3. In a 3-quart casserole, mix the rice and barley with the onion, 2 tablespoons of the reserved seasoning mix, thyme, pepper, and rosemary. Stir in the stock.
4. Cover and bake for 45 minutes, or until tender. Fluff with a fork. Let stand, covered, for 5 minutes before serving.

LEMONS

They are a welcome addition to salads, vegetable dishes, desserts, beverages ~ even poultry. Just-squeezed lemon juice mixed with chopped parsley can be as satisfying as a butter sauce. And who can resist fresh lemonade (page 141), the stuff of so many childhood memories. Yet the lemon's power only begins in the kitchen. The fruit has long been used in many home remedies, as a bleach and an astringent, in hair-care potions, and in perfumes.

*Bringing the past into the
present: These antique
hollow utensil handles have
been entwined with
flattened silver-plated spoons
and transformed
into clever little bud vases.*

Beggar's Purses

SERVES 4

Tied with a strip of leek to resemble a hobo's pouch, a beggar's purse actually holds a tempting combination of wild mushrooms and wild rice. You can experiment with other fillings for the pastry, using whatever vegetables are in season.

I tablespoon clarified butter
I cup sliced morel mushrooms
I teaspoon chopped garlic
¼ cup Madeira
I tablespoon chopped chives
½ cup cooked wild rice

4 sheets phyllo pastry, thawed if frozen
4 tablespoons unsalted butter, melted
Leek tops, cut in 4 ribbons and blanched

1. In a medium-size skillet, melt the butter and sauté the morel mushrooms and garlic. Add the Madeira and boil gently until the wine evaporates. Stir in the chives.

2. Cool the vegetables to room temperature. Stir in the rice.

3. Preheat the oven to 425°F.

4. Keep the phyllo pastry you are not working with covered with a damp tea towel. Brush a sheet of phyllo pastry with melted butter. Top with a second sheet of pastry and brush with butter again. Continue layering with the remaining pastry sheets, brushing each with butter. Cut the pastry in half both lengthwise and crosswise to form four rectangles.

5. Working quickly, spoon a quarter of the wild rice filling onto the center of each dough rectangle. Bring up all sides of each rectangle and, using a ribbon of leek, tie the pastry in a hobo-style package. Brush the pastry bundles all over with melted butter. Place them on an unbuttered baking sheet.

6. Bake the bundles until they are browned and crisp, 8 to 10 minutes.

NOTE: To make the bundles in advance, prepare and bake as above. Cool to room temperature. Arrange them on a baking sheet, cover, and refrigerate for up to 6 hours. At serving time, uncover and bake them in a preheated 375°F oven for 10 minutes, or until they are heated through.

James River Wild Rice Pancakes

MAKES 8 OR 9 PANCAKES

1 cup cooked, drained wild rice

1 scallion with top, minced

½ small red bell pepper, minced

1 cup all-purpose flour

1 teaspoon baking powder

1 cup milk

¼ cup vegetable oil

Salt and pepper to taste

1. In a small bowl, combine the wild rice, scallion, and red pepper. Mix well and set aside.

2. Sift the flour and baking powder into a large bowl. Add the milk and vegetable oil and season with salt and pepper. Whisk until blended. Fold in the wild rice mixture.

3. Heat a griddle and brush the surface with vegetable oil. Using a ¼ cup measure, drop pancakes onto the hot griddle. Cook until bubbles appear all over the tops of the pancakes and the bottoms are browned. Turn the pancakes over and cook until they are golden brown and done in the center.

Timbales of Macaroni & Cheese

SERVES 8

4 eggs

1 cup heavy cream

1 cup (4 ounces) grated cheddar cheese

⅓ cup chopped scallion tops

4 cups cooked, drained macaroni

Salt, pepper, paprika, and cayenne pepper to taste

1. Preheat the oven to 350°F. Generously butter eight 6-ounce custard cups.

2. In a large bowl, whisk the eggs until well beaten. Whisk in the cream, cheese, and scallion tops until blended. Fold in the macaroni and season to taste with the spices.

3. Spoon the mixture into the prepared custard cups. Arrange the cups in a large shallow baking pan, and pour hot water around them to a depth of 1 inch.

4. Bake the timbales for 40 to 45 minutes, until they are set in the center.

5. Remove the cups from the water bath. Run a narrow metal spatula around the edges of the cups to loosen, then gently slip a spatula under the bottoms of the timbales to remove them from the cups.

FAMILY PRIDE

Wherever they appear, monograms tell a story ~ of a relationship, perhaps, or even an entire family history. Their permanence on treasured items also speaks of a faith in the future as well as their acknowledgment of the past. While we most often picture linens when we think of monograms, they also adorn china, flatware, samplers, pillows, box and jar lids, even thimbles.

Herbed Focaccia

New York baker and teacher Lauren Groveman treats her family to homemade croissants or muffins every day. To her, no table is set without fresh bread, and she believes that even a first-time baker can make better bread than store-bought varieties. To give focaccia an authentic crust, she recommends buying square terracotta tiles for the oven.

FOCACCIA DOUGH

Pinch of sugar, plus ½ tablespoon additional sugar

I (¼-ounce) package active dry yeast

1½ tablespoons extra virgin olive oil

½ cup very finely chopped yellow onion

2 tablespoons chopped basil

½ tablespoon chopped thyme

I teaspoon chopped rosemary

½ teaspoon chopped sage

Freshly ground black pepper to taste

½ cup warm (110°F) milk

2 cups all-purpose flour

2 tablespoons chopped, pitted Kalamata olives (optional)

½ tablespoon salt

1½ to 2 cups bread flour

TOPPING

1½ tablespoons extra virgin olive oil

I cup thin strips yellow onion

I teaspoon chopped thyme

I teaspoon chopped rosemary

Freshly ground black pepper to taste

¼ cup cornmeal

Extra virgin olive oil

Coarse salt and freshly ground pepper to taste

1. To make the focaccia dough, butter the large bowl of an electric mixer. Brush a 12 by 7½ by 2-inch baking dish with olive oil.

2. In a small bowl, combine ¼ cup of warm (110°F) water and a pinch of sugar. Sprinkle the yeast on top and let it stand until it dissolves and bubbles, 8 to 10 minutes.

3. Meanwhile, heat 1½ tablespoons olive oil in a small skillet and sauté the chopped onion over medium heat until soft. Stir in the basil, ½ tablespoon thyme, I teaspoon rosemary, and the sage, and pepper to taste. Cook, stirring gently, for I minute. Pour into the buttered bowl.

4. Stir in the warm milk, ½ cup plus 2 tablespoons of warm water, ½ tablespoon of sugar, and the dissolved yeast. Add the all-purpose flour. Beat at high speed for 3 minutes. Stir in the olives, if desired.

5. Cover the dough and let it rise in a warm place until it has doubled in size, about 30 minutes.

6. Brush a large bowl with some olive oil.

7. Stir ½ tablespoon salt into the dough. Slowly stir in some of the bread flour with a wooden spoon until the dough forms a ball. Turn the dough out onto a well-floured surface. Knead the dough until it is

smooth and elastic, about 8 to 10 minutes, adding enough flour to keep the dough from sticking.

8. Place the dough in the oiled bowl, turning once to coat the surface. Cover and let it rise in a warm place until it has doubled in size, about 45 minutes.

9. While the dough is rising, make the topping: Heat 1½ tablespoons olive oil in a skillet and sauté the onion strips over medium heat until soft. Add 1 teaspoon thyme, 1 teaspoon rosemary, and pepper to taste. Cook, stirring gently, for 1 minute. Remove the skillet from the heat.

10. Sprinkle the prepared baking dish with 2 tablespoons of the cornmeal. Do not shake out the excess cornmeal. Turn the dough into the center of the dish and sprinkle it with the remaining cornmeal. Gently push the dough out toward the sides of the dish, pulling lightly on the dough to spread across the baking dish. If the dough tears, pinch it back together. The dough should fill the dish evenly. Using a brush, dab the top of the dough with olive oil. Using a fork, lightly prick the dough at 1-inch intervals.

11. Spoon the topping over the dough, spreading to within 1 inch of the edges. Sprinkle with coarse salt and freshly ground pepper.

12. Let the dough rise, uncovered, in a warm place until it has doubled in size, about 45 minutes. Preheat the oven to 425°F.

13. Bake the focaccia for 30 minutes. Run a knife around the edge of the dish to loosen the bread. Using two spatulas, remove it to cool on a rack. Cut the focaccia in squares or diamonds.

Corn Bread with Fresh Corn

MAKES 18 TO 24 SQUARES

1½ cups yellow cornmeal

1 cup unbleached all-purpose flour

¼ cup sugar

1 teaspoon baking soda

1 teaspoon baking powder

¼ teaspoon salt

½ cup vegetable oil

2 eggs, lightly beaten

1 (16-ounce) container sour cream

½ cup fresh corn kernels or thawed frozen corn

¼ cup minced red bell pepper

1. Preheat the oven to 375°F. Butter a 13 by 9 by 2-inch baking pan.

2. Sift the cornmeal, flour, sugar, baking soda, baking powder, and salt into a large bowl. Make a well in the center of the dry ingredients. Pour in the oil, eggs, and sour cream. Stir the batter quickly to blend. Fold in the corn and red pepper.

3. Pour the batter into the prepared pan. Let it stand for 4 minutes.

4. Bake for 25 minutes, or until it is golden brown and the top springs back when lightly touched in the center. Cool the corn bread in the pan set on a rack for 10 minutes.

5. Cut into squares and serve the corn bread warm.

WHOLE-WHEAT FRENCH BREAD

MAKES 2 LOAVES

Cornmeal

4 to 4 ½ cups bread flour

3 (¼-ounce) packages active dry yeast

2 teaspoons salt

2 teaspoons sugar

½ tablespoon honey or malt syrup

2⅔ cups whole-wheat flour

1. Line two baking sheets with parchment paper. Sprinkle the paper evenly with cornmeal. Generously butter a large bowl. Set aside.

2. In the large bowl of an electric mixer, combine 2½ cups of the bread flour with the yeast, salt, and sugar. Mix well. Add 2⅓ cups of warm (110°F) water and the honey. Beat at medium speed for 2 minutes, scraping the side of the bowl occasionally.

3. Add 1 cup of the bread flour. Beat at low speed to blend, then at high speed for 2 minutes.

4. Gradually stir in the whole-wheat flour by hand. Stir in enough of the remaining bread flour to make a moderately stiff dough.

5. Turn the dough out on a floured surface. Knead it for 10 minutes, until it is smooth and very elastic. Place the dough in the buttered bowl, turning it once to coat the whole surface.

6. Cover the bowl and let the dough rise in a warm place until it has doubled in size, about 45 minutes.

7. Punch the dough down. Turn it out on a floured surface. Cover it and let it rest for 10 minutes.

8. Divide the dough in half. Roll or pat each half to a 12 by 8-inch rectangle. Roll the dough up jelly-roll fashion starting at a long side. Gently pinch together the edges and ends to seal. Place the dough diagonally, seam side down, on the prepared sheets.

9. Cover the dough and let it rise in a warm place until it has doubled in size again, about 30 minutes. Preheat the oven to 400°F.

10. Bake the bread for 10 minutes. Reduce the oven temperature to 350°F and bake for 20 to 25 minutes more. Remove the loaves from the baking sheets and cool on racks.

Herbed Gougères

MAKES 3 RINGS

Though they are made with cream-puff pastry dough, gougères are savory, not sweet. In this recipe, the dough is flavored with Gruyère and fresh herbs and baked in a ring shape. To make bite-size puffs, drop the dough by a level ½ tablespoon one inch apart on prepared baking sheets then bake for 18 to 20 minutes. This recipe will yield about seven dozen individual puffs. Gougères are perfect hors d'oeuvres to serve with cocktails.

½ cup (I stick) unsalted
  butter, cut up

¼ teaspoon salt

I cup all-purpose flour

4 eggs

I cup coarsely grated Gruyère

I tablespoon chopped parsley

I tablespoon chopped fresh dill

I tablespoon chopped
  fresh chives

1. Line 3 baking sheets with foil. Butter the foil. Preheat the oven to 425°F.
2. In a heavy medium-size saucepan, combine the butter, salt, and I cup water. Bring the mixture to a boil, stirring to melt the butter. Remove the pan from the heat.
3. Add the flour to the butter mixture all at once and beat vigorously with a wooden spoon until the mixture is well blended. Cook the dough over medium heat, stirring constantly, until it becomes stiff and pulls away from the side of the pan. Remove the pan from the heat.
4. Beat in the eggs, one at a time, beating well after each addition.

Stir in ⅔ cup Gruyère and the chopped parsley, dill, and chives.
5. Shape the dough into 3 rings. Working with one third of the dough, drop 14 mounds from a level tablespoon ⅜ inch apart in a circle about 10 inches in diameter on a prepared baking sheet. Repeat with the remaining dough, making 2 additional rings. Sprinkle all the rings with the remaining ⅓ cup Gruyère.
6. Bake the rings in the preheated oven for 23 to 25 minutes, until the pastry is puffed and golden brown.
7. Remove the rings from the baking sheets. Cool them on wire racks. Serve the gougères at room temperature.

TRUE BLUE

From rich cobalt to the pale blue of a summer sky, from landscapes to still-lifes often as finely detailed as a painting ~ these are the hallmarks of fine English Staffordshire china. Staffordshire was produced in five towns in north-central England, called The Potteries, in the eighteenth and nineteenth centuries. By far the most popular and prized pattern was Blue Willow, introduced by Thomas Minton in the 1780s.

47

Centerpieces

A fashionable, well-to-do Victorian host might have served dinner guests a fish course, an entree of poultry, and then a roast ~ in addition to appetizers, a soup, vegetables, and sweets for dessert. Today, for family or for company, any one course of fish or meat is likely to be plenty. And sometimes, it's just a poultry or seafood salad or a pasta dish that we crave.

Nasturtium Shrimp Salad

SERVES 2

2 tablespoons lemon juice

¼ cup olive oil

Salt and freshly ground pepper to taste

8 ounces shelled cooked shrimp

2 tablespoons finely chopped onion

1 small tomato, sliced

½ cucumber, sliced

Pesticide-free nasturtium leaves

Leaf lettuce

Pesticide-free nasturtium flowers, for garnish

1. Put the lemon juice in a small bowl. Whisk in the olive oil in a thin stream. Season with salt and pepper. Add the shrimp and onion. Toss the salad lightly, then cover and refrigerate for 15 minutes to let the flavors blend.

2. Serve the shrimp salad, tomato, and cucumber on the nasturtium and lettuce leaves and garnish with the nasturtium flowers.

LOBSTER SALAD WITH FRESH MANGO

SERVES 4 TO 6

MANGO SAUCE

1 tablespoon olive oil

3 garlic cloves, crushed

2 shallots, chopped

1 serrano chili pepper, seeded

1 cup dry white wine

3 large mangoes, about
    12 ounces each

2 cups fish or chicken stock

1 teaspoon chopped basil

1 teaspoon chopped cilantro

MINT VINAIGRETTE

Juice of ½ lemon

¼ cup olive oil

1 teaspoon chopped mint

Salt and pepper to taste

3 cups cubed cooked lobster

6 cups torn field greens

1 tomato, peeled, seeded, and
    diced, for garnish

1. To make the mango sauce, heat 1 tablespoon olive oil in a heavy large saucepan over medium heat. Add the garlic, shallots, and serrano pepper. Cover with a buttered round of waxed paper, then with the lid. Cook the vegetables slowly so they do not color, for 3 to 5 minutes.

2. Pour in the wine. Reduce the liquid over high heat until the pan is almost dry.

3. Puree one of the mangoes.

4. Add the fish stock, mango puree, basil, and cilantro to the vegetable mixture. Bring to a boil. Reduce the heat and simmer for 30 minutes. Strain the stock, discarding the solids.

5. Return the liquid to the saucepan. Peel and cube the remaining mangoes. Add that to the liquid and bring it to a boil. Reduce the heat and simmer until the mango is tender, 3 to 5 minutes.

6. Puree the sauce in a blender, then strain it into a bowl. Cover and refrigerate for 4 hours.

7. To make the mint vinaigrette, whisk together the lemon juice, olive oil, and mint in a small bowl until they are blended. Season with salt and pepper.

8. Just before serving, toss the lobster and field greens with the mint vinaigrette.

9. To serve, pour the mango sauce on each of 4 to 6 chilled dinner plates. Spoon the lobster salad in the center of each plate and garnish with the diced tomatoes.

Salmon with Chanterelles

SERVES 4

An island of serenity in New York City is Chanterelle, where even the walls are a soothing chanterelle color. But the sublime food prepared by chef David Waltuck will awaken the senses. This dish, though simply presented, has an intensely flavored mushroom sauce.

I tablespoon unsalted butter

12 ounces chanterelle mushrooms, sliced lengthwise

4 (6-ounce) salmon fillets or steaks, cut ¾ inch to 1 inch thick

¾ cup fish stock

¼ cup dry white wine

I tablespoon chopped shallots

2 tablespoons lemon juice

½ teaspoon Dijon mustard

¼ cup heavy cream

Salt and pepper to taste

Chopped chervil, chives, and parsley, for garnish

I. In a large skillet, melt the butter over medium heat. Add the chanterelles. Cover with a buttered round of waxed paper and the lid. Cook for 5 minutes, or until tender.
2. Remove the chanterelles with a slotted spoon, reserving the juices from the skillet.
3. Add the salmon, fish stock, wine, and shallots to the juices in the skillet. Bring to a boil, then reduce the heat to medium-low. Cover and simmer the salmon for 5 to 6 minutes on each side, until the fish flakes in the center of the thickest part when tested with a fork.

4. Remove the salmon with a slotted spatula, reserving the pan juices. Cover the salmon and keep it warm.
5. Boil the pan juices over medium-high heat until they are reduced by half. Strain and return them to the skillet. Stir in the lemon juice, mustard, and cream. Add the chanterelles. Boil the mixture gently until it is slightly thickened. Season with salt and pepper.
6. To serve, ladle the sauce over the salmon on serving plates. Sprinkle with chervil, chives, and parsley, for garnish.

Marinated Ahi Tuna Steaks

SERVES 8

MARINATED TUNA

1 (3½-ounce) jar green
    peppercorns in brine

½ cup mild honey

¼ cup olive oil

8 (8-ounce) center-cut Ahi
    tuna steaks, ¾ inch thick

Salt and freshly ground
    pepper to taste

BASIL-AVOCADO COMPOTE

3 avocados, peeled and cubed
    (3 cups)

½ cup chopped red bell pepper

½ cup chopped yellow bell
    pepper

1 small red onion, thinly sliced
    and separated in rings

Juice from 1 lime

Salt and pepper to taste

1 bunch purple basil,
    cut in julienne

YAM CHIPS

Oil for deep frying

2 medium-size yams,
    peeled and sliced crosswise
    ¹⁄₁₆ inch thick

6 tablespoons olive oil

Thyme sprigs, for garnish

1. To make the marinade, puree the green peppercorns with their brine in a food processor. Add the honey and olive oil. Process until blended.

2. Arrange the tuna steaks in a shallow baking dish. Season them with salt and pepper. Pour the marinade evenly over the tuna. Cover and refrigerate for about 8 hours, turning the steaks over at least once.

3. To make the vegetable compote, combine the avocado, red pepper, yellow pepper, and onion in a medium-size bowl. Season with lime juice and salt and pepper. Toss to mix. Add the basil and toss gently. Cover and refrigerate.

4. To make the yam chips, heat oil in a deep fryer to 375°F. Deep-fry the yam slices in small batches until they are crispy, about 1 minute. Drain them on paper towels and keep them warm.

5. Heat 3 tablespoons of olive oil in each of two large skillets over medium-high heat.

6. Drain the tuna steaks. Sauté them for 4 to 5 minutes on one side. Turn them over and cook over medium heat 4 to 5 minutes more, until they flake in the center.

7. Slice the steaks diagonally and arrange the slices in crisscross fashion down the center of 8 warm plates. Garnish with the compote, yam chips, and thyme sprigs.

SERVING UTENSILS

At a time when exquisite details mattered a great deal, serving spoons were forged for every imaginable purpose: sugar shells, gravy ladles, ice spoons, stuffing spoons, vegetable servers, and cream ladles. So ornate were they that some required a master craftsman to work a year on the mold.

Flounder in Parchment with Mixed Vegetables

SERVES 5

1 teaspoon salt

1 teaspoon finely ground black pepper

1 teaspoon dried thyme

½ pound green beans, trimmed

2 medium-size carrots, peeled

2 medium-size parsnips, peeled

5 flounder or sole fillets, about 4 ounces each

Juice of 1 lemon

½ cup unsalted butter, softened, plus 5 thin pats cold unsalted butter

15 slices onion (about 2 medium onions)

5 tablespoons thinly sliced shallots

2 tablespoons finely chopped parsley

½ cup plus 2 tablespoons dry white wine

1. In a small bowl, combine the salt, pepper, and thyme. Mix well.

2. Cut the beans, carrots, and parsnips into thin julienne about 2½ inches long.

3. Wipe the flounder with a clean, damp cloth. Squeeze a few drops of lemon juice over each fillet.

4. Cut five 18 by 15-inch sheets of parchment paper. Spread 1½ tablespoons softened butter in a 4-inch square in the center of each sheet.

5. Arrange 3 onion slices on top of the butter. Curve a fish fillet over the onion slices. Sprinkle each fillet with ½ teaspoon of the salt mixture. Divide the julienne vegetables and shallots among the packets, mounding them on top of the fish.

6. Sprinkle the packets with half the parsley. Dot each packet with 1 pat of the cold butter and sprinkle with the remaining parsley.

7. To form each pouch, bring the opposite corners of the parchment paper together over the center of the food, pleating the corners of the package in toward the center. While holding the top ends of the paper upright, drizzle 2 tablespoons white wine into each pouch. Cinch the paper together and tie each package tightly with string.

8. Set the pouches an inch apart in a single layer on a baking sheet. At this point, they can be refrigerated for up to 2 hours before cooking.

9. Preheat the oven to 400°F.

10. Place the fish packets in the oven. Increase the oven temperature to 425°F. Bake for 17 minutes, or until the fish flakes in the center when tested with a fork and the vegetables are crisp-tender.

Spaghetti Primavera

SERVES 6 TO 8

SAUTÉED TOMATOES

3 tablespoons olive oil

4 teaspoons finely chopped garlic

3 cups ripe tomatoes, cut in 1-inch cubes

6 fresh basil leaves, chopped, or 1 teaspoon dried basil

Salt and pepper to taste

SAUTÉED MUSHROOMS

1 tablespoon vegetable oil

2 cups mushrooms, thinly sliced

¼ cup parsley, finely chopped

½ teaspoon dried red pepper flakes

SAUTÉED VEGETABLES

1½ cups zucchini, quartered lengthwise and cut in 1-inch pieces

1½ cups asparagus, cut in 1-inch pieces

1½ cups green beans, cut in 1-inch pieces

1 cup bite-size broccoli florets

½ cup peas

16 pea pods

3 tablespoons olive oil

2 teaspoons finely chopped garlic

PASTA

1 pound spaghetti

CREAM SAUCE

2 tablespoons unsalted butter

¼ cup chicken broth

½ cup dry white wine

¼ cup heavy cream

⅓ cup toasted pine nuts

⅔ cup grated Parmesan

1. To make the tomatoes, heat 3 tablespoons oil in a medium-size skillet. Sauté 2 teaspoons garlic in the oil. Add the tomatoes and basil and season with salt and pepper. Cook over medium heat, stirring constantly, for 5 minutes.

2. To make the mushrooms, heat 1 tablespoon vegetable oil in another skillet and sauté the mushrooms for 2 minutes. Stir in the parsley and pepper flakes. Mix and set aside.

3. To make the vegetables, separately blanch the zucchini, asparagus, green beans, broccoli, peas, and pea pods in a large pot of boiling water until crisp-tender. Immediately plunge the vegetables into ice water. Drain.

4. In the same large pot, heat 3 tablespoons olive oil and sauté 2 teaspoons garlic. Add the blanched vegetables. Cook, tossing often, over low heat until heated through.

5. Make the pasta while the vegetables are cooking: Cook the spaghetti in a large pot of boiling water until al dente. Drain, then return the spaghetti to the pot.

6. To make the cream sauce, melt the butter over medium-low heat in a medium-size saucepan. Whisk in the chicken broth, wine, and cream until blended. Heat through.

7. To assemble, strain the tomatoes, reserving the juice and pulp separately. Set aside.

8. Pour the hot cream sauce over the spaghetti in the pot, tossing to coat. Add half the sautéed vegetables and tomato juice. Toss over medium-low heat.

9. Add the remaining sautéed vegetables, sautéed mushrooms, and pine nuts. Toss.

10. Gradually sprinkle with Parmesan, tossing to mix.

11. Serve the spaghetti in heated bowls. Spoon the sautéed tomatoes over each serving.

Pennsylvania Pasta with Fresh Mushrooms

SERVES 4

Mushroom expert Joe Czarnecki forages for the delectable varieties he uses in his kitchen at the justly famous Joe's Restaurant in Reading, Pennsylvania. This pasta dish harmonizes with just about any wild mushrooms.

3 tablespoons unsalted butter
½ cup chopped onion
¼ cup dry red wine
1 tablespoon soy sauce
1 teaspoon salt
1 teaspoon sugar
1 teaspoon minced garlic
1 teaspoon lemon juice
½ teaspoon chili powder
½ teaspoon ground coriander
¼ teaspoon pepper
1 pound fresh wild mushrooms (halve or slice large mushrooms)
1½ tablespoons cornstarch
3 cups wide egg noodles, cooked and kept hot

1. In a large skillet, melt the butter and sauté the onion over medium heat until the onion is transparent.

2. Stir in ½ cup of water and the red wine, soy sauce, salt, sugar, minced garlic, lemon juice, chili powder, coriander, and pepper. Cook and stir for 1 minute.

3. Stir in the mushrooms and bring to a simmer. Reduce the heat, cover, and simmer the sauce for 30 minutes.

4. In a small bowl, gradually stir ⅓ cup of cold water into the cornstarch until smooth. Stir that into the hot mushroom mixture. Cook, stirring constantly, over medium heat until the mixture thickens and comes to a boil.

5. Pour the mushroom sauce over the hot noodles.

CHINA

When families left their homelands for the promise that was America, they left many possessions behind. Only the best objects were chosen to make the trip, perhaps a bowl with a burnished gold rim or a beloved set of goblets. Now, more than a century later, those handed-down prized pieces may grow even more important as they're mixed with new purchases and carefully placed on our tables.

Chicken Potpie with Parsley Crust

SERVES 6

Parsley Pastry

2 cups all-purpose flour

2 tablespoons finely chopped parsley

½ teaspoon salt

⅔ cup shortening

Stewed Chicken

I (3-pound) broiler-fryer chicken, cut up

¼ cup chopped celery leaves

3 tablespoons chopped fresh tarragon, or I tablespoon dried

I bay leaf

I teaspoon salt

¼ teaspoon pepper

Cream Sauce

4 tablespoons unsalted butter

I medium-size onion, chopped

⅓ cup all-purpose flour

½ teaspoon salt

¼ teaspoon pepper

I cup heavy cream or milk

Vegetable Filling

I cup diced cooked carrots

I cup cooked peas

I cup diced cooked potatoes

I egg yolk

I. To make the pastry, combine 2 cups flour, the parsley, and ½ teaspoon salt in a large bowl. With a pastry blender or two knives, cut in the shortening until the mixture resembles peas.

2. Add 6 to 7 tablespoons ice water, a tablespoon at a time, tossing with a fork until all is moistened. Gather the dough into a ball and shape it into a disk. Wrap the pastry and refrigerate for at least 30 minutes.

3. To make the chicken, combine the chicken, celery leaves, tarragon, bay leaf, I teaspoon salt, and pepper in a large saucepan. Add enough cold water to cover.

4. Bring the water to a boil over high heat. Reduce the heat, cover, and simmer for 45 minutes to I hour, until the chicken is very tender.

5. Remove the chicken with tongs and set aside. Strain and refrigerate the stock. When the chicken is cool enough to handle, discard the skin and remove the meat from the bones. Cut the meat into bite-size pieces. Wrap and refrigerate them.

6. To make the cream sauce, skim the fat from the top of the cold stock. In a medium-size saucepan, melt the butter. Add the onion and sauté until transparent, 3 to 5 minutes. Stir in ⅓ cup flour, ½ teaspoon salt, and the pepper. Whisk in 2 cups of stock and the cream. Cook, stirring constantly, over medium heat, until the sauce comes to a boil and thickens, 10 to 15 minutes. Remove from the heat.

7. In a 10- or 11-inch round or square casserole with a 3-quart capacity, combine the chicken, carrots, peas, and potatoes. Pour in the sauce and mix gently.

8. Preheat the oven to 375°F.

9. On a lightly floured surface, roll

the dough out 2 inches larger than the top of the casserole. Moisten the edge of the casserole with water. Place the dough on the casserole, folding the edges under and crimping to the top edge. (The crust should be suspended above the filling, not on it.) Cut several vents in the crust.
10. Beat the egg yolk with I tablespoon water. Brush the crust with the egg yolk wash.
II. Bake for 40 to 50 minutes, until the crust is golden and the sauce is bubbling.

CHICKEN SALAD WITH GINGER MAYONNAISE

SERVES 6

½ cup mayonnaise

½ cup sour cream

I tablespoon dry white wine

I teaspoon ground ginger

½ teaspoon dry mustard

3 to 4 tablespoons minced crystallized ginger

4 cups cubed cooked chicken

2 cups chopped celery

I cup julienne sticks jicama or water chestnuts

I pear, peeled, cored, and cubed (I cup)

3 to 4 scallions, thinly sliced on the diagonal

¾ cup toasted whole almonds, for garnish

I. In a small bowl, whisk together the mayonnaise and sour cream. Whisk in the white wine, ground ginger, and dry mustard. Stir in the crystallized ginger.
2. In a bowl, combine the chicken, celery, jicama, pear, and scallions. Spoon the ginger mayonnaise over the salad and toss gently. Cover and refrigerate for at least 2 hours.
3. To serve, garnish the salad with the toasted almonds.

SMOKED TURKEY SALAD

SERVES 6 TO 8

MAPLE DIJON DRESSING

⅓ cup sherry wine vinegar

3 tablespoons maple syrup

2 tablespoons whole-grain Dijon mustard

Salt and pepper to taste

⅔ cup canola oil

SMOKED TURKEY SALAD

6 small yams, about I inch in diameter

2 tablespoons olive oil

I½ pounds smoked turkey, cut in julienne

½ cup chopped celery

½ cup dried cranberries

GINGERROOT

Available fresh, dried and ground, pickled, and crystallized, ginger can appear almost anywhere in the meal. Fresh gingerroot, firm and knobby, is ubiquitous in Chinese stir fries, and the foods of the Caribbean (where it was introduced by the Spanish explorers), North Africa, Great Britain, and India frequently call for ginger. Ground ginger flavors dozens of sweets, and the best-known of them, gingerbread, is many centuries old.

1. To make the dressing, combine the sherry vinegar, maple syrup, mustard, and salt and pepper in a medium-size bowl. Slowly whisk in the canola oil.

2. To make the salad, combine the yams and enough water to cover by 2 inches in a large pot. Bring to a boil, reduce the heat, cover, and boil gently for 20 to 25 minutes until just tender. Drain the yams. Refrigerate until cool.

3. Preheat the oven to 375°F. Lightly butter a baking sheet.

4. Peel the yams and cut them in ¼-inch slices. Arrange the slices in a single layer on the prepared baking sheet. Brush with the olive oil.

5. Bake for 15 minutes. Cool on the baking sheet set on a rack for about 45 minutes.

6. In a large bowl, combine the turkey, celery, and cranberries. Whisk the dressing and drizzle some over the salad, mixing to coat.

7. Carefully add the yams. Drizzle with more dressing. Gently fold in the yams. Cover and refrigerate the salad until serving time.

BROILED GINGER CHICKEN

SERVES 4

As Victorian cookbook writer Isabella Beeton noted, ginger is among the most widely used flavorings, both for sweets and jams as well as for savory dishes like this ginger chicken from Pittsburgh journalist Marlene Parrish.

I (3-pound) broiler-fryer chicken, quartered

I-inch piece peeled gingerroot, finely chopped

I garlic clove, finely chopped

½ to ¾ teaspoon pepper

½ teaspoon dried thyme

¼ teaspoon salt

½ bay leaf, crumbled

¼ cup lemon juice

2 tablespoons vegetable oil

1. Arrange the chicken pieces, skin side up, in a single layer in a shallow baking dish.

2. In a screw-top jar, combine the gingerroot, garlic, pepper, thyme, salt, bay leaf, lemon juice, and oil. Cover and shake until blended. Pour the marinade over the chicken.

3. Cover and refrigerate the chicken pieces for 8 hours or overnight, turning them over in the marinade occasionally.

4. Preheat an electric broiler. (It is not necessary to preheat a gas broiler.) Arrange the chicken pieces, skin side down, in the bottom of a broiler pan without a rack.

5. Broil the chicken 4 to 5 inches from the heat for 15 minutes. Turn and broil 6 to 8 minutes, until the juices run clear. (The chicken may also be cooked on a barbecue grill.)

COUNTRY HERBED CHICKEN

SERVES 4

¼ to ½ cup unsalted butter, softened

1 tablespoon chopped parsley

1 tablespoon chopped fresh thyme, or 1 teaspoon dried

2 teaspoons chopped fresh rosemary, or ½ teaspoon dried

Grated zest and fruit of 1 lemon

Salt and pepper to taste

1 (3½-pound) whole broiler-fryer chicken

1. Preheat the oven to 350°F. In a small bowl, cream the butter. Stir in the parsley, thyme, rosemary, and lemon zest, and season with salt and pepper.
2. Spread the butter mixture over the chicken. Spoon any extra inside the body cavity. Quarter the lemon and place it in the body cavity. Place the chicken in a shallow baking pan.
3. Roast the chicken for 1½ to 1¾ hours, until a thermometer inserted between the leg and thigh registers 185°F.

ZINFANDEL MARINATED CHICKEN

SERVES 4

1½ cups Zinfandel or other dry red wine

¾ cup olive oil

3 tablespoons soy sauce or tamari sauce

1 tablespoon Worcestershire sauce

1 tablespoon Dijon mustard

Pepper to taste

1 (3-pound) broiler-fryer chicken, cut up

1. In a screw-top jar, combine the wine, oil, soy sauce, Worcestershire sauce, mustard, and pepper. Cover and shake until blended.
2. Put the chicken in a large plastic bag set in a shallow pan. Pour the marinade over the chicken, forcing as much marinade up around the chicken as possible. Tie the bag closed tightly.
3. Refrigerate the chicken for 4 to 6 hours, turning the bag over once.
4. Grill or broil the chicken, turning it often, until the juices run clear. Discard the marinade and arrange the chicken on a platter.

LEMON-GINGER CORNISH HENS

SERVES 6

6 lemons

2 inches gingerroot, chopped

½ cup honey

⅓ cup cooking oil

1 stalk lemon grass, split lengthwise (optional)

Salt and pepper to taste

3 (1½-pound) Cornish hens, thawed

⅓ cup packed light brown sugar

2 pounds onions, sliced

Lemon slices, for garnish

1. To make the marinade, grate the zest from 3 lemons and juice all 6 lemons. In a medium-size bowl, whisk together the grated lemon zest, lemon juice, gingerroot, honey, and oil. Add the lemon grass. Season with salt and pepper.

2. Split the hens in half lengthwise, and arrange in a single layer in a large plastic bag set in a shallow roasting pan. Pour the marinade over the birds. Tie the bag closed tightly, pressing as much marinade as possible up around the hens.

3. Refrigerate for 12 hours or overnight, turning the bag over once.

4. Preheat the oven to 375°F. Drain the hens, reserving the marinade. Discard the lemon grass. Arrange the hens skin side up in the same baking pan. Pour half the marinade over the birds.

5. Bake the hens for 35 minutes, then baste them with the pan juice. Continue baking for an additional 25 minutes, or until the juices run clear when the thighs are pierced.

6. While the hens are roasting, make the glazed onions: Heat the remaining half of the marinade in a heavy large skillet. Add the brown sugar and onions.

7. Bring the mixture to a boil, then reduce the heat to medium. Cook, stirring occasionally, for 35 minutes, until the onions are soft and caramelized.

8. To make the sauce, remove the hens to a serving platter, reserving the pan juices. Keep the hens warm.

9. Set the roasting pan with pan juices over two burners. Bring to a boil and boil until the pan juices are just starting to brown and are reduced by about half; watch closely toward the end of the cooking time.

10. On individual serving plates, arrange the hens on a bed of onions. Whisk the hot pan juices and spoon over the hens. Garnish with the lemon slices.

Roast Loin of Pork with Fruit, Corn Bread & Sausage Stuffing

SERVES 6 TO 8

½ pound plums, pitted and sliced (1½ cups)

½ pound dried fruit, such as apricots, pears, and prunes, chopped

1 cup Champagne, preferably blanc de noirs

1½ cups corn bread crumbs

¾ cup chopped walnuts

10 ounces ground pork sausage, cooked, drained, and crumbled

3 tablespoons chopped fresh basil, or 1 tablespoon dried, plus additional for gravy

4 tablespoons unsalted butter, melted

2 tablespoons brandy

1 (4-pound) boneless pork loin roast (single loin)

Salt and pepper to taste

1 cup chicken broth

1. In a medium-size bowl, macerate the plums and dried fruit in the Champagne for several hours. Drain, reserving the liquid.

2. In a large bowl, toss together the drained fruit, corn bread crumbs, walnuts, sausage, and basil. Drizzle with butter and brandy, and toss until moistened.

3. Butter a 1-quart casserole and spoon half the stuffing into it. Cover and refrigerate.

4. Preheat the oven to 350°F.

5. Butterfly the roast by cutting it almost in half lengthwise, starting on one side of the roast and cutting through both ends and almost through to the opposite side. Fold back the top of the roast so it lies flat, butterfly fashion.

6. Spoon the remaining stuffing on the bottom half of the roast. Cover by folding the top half back over the stuffing to reassemble the roast. Tie it securely with cotton string. Arrange the roast on a rack in a shallow roasting pan and season it with salt and pepper.

7. Roast for 2 to 2¼ hours, until a thermometer inserted in the center registers 160° to 170°F. Bake the covered casserole of stuffing alongside the roast during the last 30 minutes of baking time.

8. Remove the roast to a warm platter, reserving the drippings in the pan. Tent the roast with foil.

9. Remove the rack from the roasting pan. Pour the fruit-macerating liquid and the broth into the pan. Season with salt, pepper, and basil to taste. Bring to a boil and boil gently until it is slightly reduced. Strain and skim off the fat.

10. Slice the roast and ladle the gravy over the slices.

BEEF STEW WITH BOUQUET GARNI

SERVES 6

MARINATED BEEF

1 garlic clove

10 black peppercorns, crushed

8 whole allspice berries

1 teaspoon salt

1 cup dry red wine

3 pounds beef rump roast, cut in 1-inch cubes

BOUQUET GARNI

1 bay leaf, 1 sprig thyme, 4 black peppercorns, and 1 garlic clove

BEEF STEW

3 tablespoons olive oil

2 cups beef bouillon

3 medium-size carrots, peeled and quartered

12 small white onions, peeled

3 medium-size turnips, pared and quartered

12 white mushroom caps

1 (10-ounce) package frozen peas

Salt and pepper to taste

Chopped parsley, for garnish

1. To make the marinated beef, combine 1 garlic clove, crushed peppercorns, allspice, salt, and wine in a deep bowl. Stir to dissolve the salt.

2. Add the beef cubes, pressing them down into the marinade to immerse them as much as possible. Cover and let marinate in the refrigerator for at least 1 hour.

3. Remove the beef and garlic from the marinade with a slotted spoon, reserving the marinade. Pat the beef and garlic dry on paper towels.

4. To make the bouquet garni, tie the bay leaf, thyme, 4 peppercorns, and 1 garlic clove in cheesecloth.

5. To make the beef stew, heat the olive oil and the garlic in a 6-quart nonreactive ovenproof pot over medium-high heat. Add the beef in two batches, searing it on all sides until it is deep brown. Return all the beef to the pot.

6. Pour in the reserved marinade and beef bouillon. Add the bouquet garni. Bring to a boil and boil gently for 10 minutes. Reduce the heat and simmer for 30 minutes.

7. Preheat the oven to 350°F.

8. Layer the carrots, onions, and turnips, and then the mushrooms on the meat mixture in the pot.

9. Cover the pot and bake for 1½ hours, or until the meat and the vegetables are tender.

10. Remove the bouquet garni. Stir in the frozen peas. Season with salt and pepper. Cover and bake for 4 minutes, until the peas are cooked.

11. Spoon the stew and cooking juices into individual serving bowls. Sprinkle with the chopped parsley.

Sweet Indulgences

The effort that goes into a homemade dessert is nearly always rewarded by the pleasure it brings. Whether simple or complex, sweets touch us in some basic way. We all love to indulge occasionally in a sweet made by hand with high-quality ingredients.

Summer Pudding

SERVES 6

In British parlance, dessert is referred to as "the pudding course." The regal Summer Pudding, a centuries-old favorite, should be served only when the fruits are at their peak, according to culinary historian Michelle Berriedale-Johnson, who provided this recipe.

8 cups fresh red summer fruits, such as raspberries, blackberries, red currants, and strawberries

2 tablespoons sugar, plus additional to taste

8 to 10 thin slices white or whole-wheat bread, crusts removed

½ cup heavy cream

Pesticide-free lilacs, for garnish

1. In a large saucepan, gently mix the fruit and sugar with ½ cup of water. Bring the mixture to a boil, reduce the heat, and cover. Cook until the fruit is tender but not mushy, 6 to 15 minutes, depending on the fruits. Make sure the mixture does not boil over. Add more sugar to taste.

2. Drain the juice into a pie plate and set aside the fruit. Soak both sides of each slice of bread in the fruit juice. Use 6 slices of the bread to line a 1½-quart bowl, overlap-ping them to make a solid shell and allowing the edges to rise above the edge of the bowl.

3. Spoon the fruit into the shell and smooth the top. Fold the edges of bread down over the fruit. Make a lid of soaked bread over the fruit, tearing the slices of bread to fit.

4. Cover the pudding with a plate that fits just inside the bowl. Place a can or other heavy weight on the plate to compress the pudding. Place the bowl in a pie plate to catch any

juices that overflow. Refrigerate the pudding for 24 hours.

5. To serve, remove the weight. Hold the plate in place and pour off any juice. Remove the plate. Loosen the edge of the pudding with a knife, then invert it onto a serving dish.

6. Beat the cream until it holds its shape, sweetening it with a little sugar, if desired. Spoon cream on the pudding, allowing it to drift down the side. Sprinkle lilac blossoms over the cream. Serve the pudding in wedges.

CHERRY COBBLER

SERVES 6

1 (16-ounce) can unsweetened pitted tart red cherries or 1 (16-ounce) package frozen dry-pack pitted tart red cherries, thawed (with juice)

½ cup plus 3 tablespoons sugar

1 tablespoon cornstarch

½ teaspoon vanilla extract

1¼ cups all-purpose flour

1½ teaspoons baking powder

¼ teaspoon baking soda

1 egg, beaten

½ cup buttermilk

½ cup (1 stick) unsalted butter, melted

Vanilla sugar (see Note)

Heavy cream, for garnish

1. Preheat the oven to 375°F.

2. Drain the cherries, reserving ¾ cup of juice. If necessary, add water to the juice to equal ¾ cup.

3. In a small saucepan, combine ½ cup of the sugar and all the cornstarch. Mix well until no lumps remain. Stir in the reserved cherry juice. Cook the mixture over medium-high heat, stirring constantly, until it begins to boil and thickens slightly. Remove the pan from the heat. Stir in the vanilla extract and cherries. Cover and keep warm.

4. In a medium-size bowl, combine the flour, the remaining 3 tablespoons sugar, the baking powder, and the baking soda. Mix well. Make a well in the center of the dry ingredients. Add the egg, buttermilk, and butter. Stir quickly just until the batter is moistened. The batter will look lumpy.

5. Pour the warm cherry filling into an 8-inch round baking dish. Add large spoonfuls of the batter to cover the fruit completely. Sprinkle the batter with vanilla sugar.

6. Bake for 25 to 30 minutes, until the topping is lightly browned. Serve warm with cream.

NOTE: Vanilla sugar adds a rich layer of flavor to many foods. To make it, split a vanilla bean lengthwise. Bury the bean in 1 pound of sugar in a quart jar. Cover the jar and wait a week before using.

Apple Almond Tartlets

MAKES 16 TARTLETS

Apples and almonds are among the traditional ingredients for winter desserts in Provence, where this recipe originates. These tart shells, however, can hold any fruits you have on hand. Try a mixture of berries or, in the fall, sautéed pears.

1¼ cups all-purpose flour

4 tablespoons cold unsalted butter, cut in small pieces, plus 4 more tablespoons

1 tablespoon confectioners' sugar

1 egg yolk

6 Granny Smith apples, peeled and cored

Juice of 1 lemon

½ cup granulated sugar

¼ cup sliced almonds or chopped walnuts, toasted

Crème Fraîche (page 187), for garnish

1. Preheat the oven to 400°F.

2. In the bowl of a food processor, combine the flour, the 4 tablespoons of cut-up butter, and the confectioners' sugar. Pulse with on/off turns until the mixture resembles coarse meal.

3. Add the egg yolk. With the processor running, gradually add 1 to 2 tablespoons of ice water until the dough begins to pull away from the side of the bowl and form a ball.

4. Flatten the dough into a disk. Roll it out on a well-floured surface or between two sheets of waxed paper until thin.

5. Cut 16 dough circles to fit 3-inch round tartlet molds, rerolling the pastry as necessary. Press the dough into the molds and trim the edges. Prick the dough all over with a fork. (If the pastry gets too soft, refrigerate it until it is firm.) Arrange the molds on a baking sheet.

6. Bake the tartlet shells for 8 to 10 minutes, until slightly browned. Cool on a rack. Remove the shells from the molds and cool completely.

7. Meanwhile, slice the apples ½ inch thick. Toss the slices with the lemon juice in a large bowl.

8. Melt 2 tablespoons of the remaining butter in a large heavy skillet over moderately high heat. Add half the apples. Sprinkle with half the granulated sugar. Sauté for 10 to 12 minutes, until the apples are tender and golden brown.

9. Repeat with the remaining butter, apples, and sugar.

10. Fill each tartlet shell with several slices of apple and top with a sprinkling of almonds. Serve warm. Garnish each tartlet with a spoonful of crème fraîche.

Pear Raspberry Tart

SERVES 6 TO 8

If you'd like to know if sweets are the way to win over a sweetheart, this pretty dessert may be the one to try. The recipe comes from Diane Margaritis of Diane's Bakery in Roslyn, New York.

Charlotte's Piecrust
(page 188)

ALMOND FILLING

4 ounces blanched almonds, ground (1 cup)

½ cup sugar

1 egg, plus 1 egg yolk

1 tablespoon light rum

¼ teaspoon almond extract

4 tablespoons unsalted butter, melted

FRUIT FILLING

2 pounds pears (3 very large, such as Comice, or 4 large, such as Bartlett)

¼ cup sugar

2 tablespoons lemon juice

½ cup fresh raspberries

APRICOT GLAZE

½ cup apricot preserves, pressed through a sieve

2 tablespoons light rum

1. Line a 9-inch tart pan with a removable bottom with the pastry. Crimp the edges. Refrigerate the pastry for 1 hour.

2. Preheat the oven to 350°F.

3. To make the filling, process the almonds, ½ cup sugar, the egg and egg yolk, 1 tablespoon rum, the almond extract, and the butter in the bowl of a food processor until smooth. Spread the almond filling in the shell.

4. To prepare the fruit, peel, quarter, and core the pears. Toss the pear quarters with ¼ cup sugar and the lemon juice. Cut each quarter into several slices.

5. Starting at the outer edge of the tart, fan the pear slices in a circle over the almond filling, overlapping the slices and making several layers of slices. Arrange a few small pear slices in the center of the pan. Place the tart pan on a baking sheet.

6. Bake for 65 to 75 minutes, until the filling and crust are golden brown. Cool the tart on a rack.

7. Mound the fresh raspberries in the center of the tart.

8. To glaze the tart, combine the strained preserves and 2 tablespoons rum in a small bowl. Brush the glaze over the pears and raspberries.

FRUIT BARQUETTES

MAKES 30 BARQUETTES

Although time-consuming to prepare, fruit barquettes are beautiful little boat-shaped pastries, often served as a trio with three different fillings. You can also make the barquettes with a savory pastry and fill them with salads of egg or seafood after the shells are baked.

SWEET PASTRY

2 cups all-purpose flour

¾ cup confectioners' sugar

Pinch of salt

7 tablespoons unsalted butter, cut in small pieces

2 eggs

CRANBERRY FILLING

2 tablespoons unsalted butter

Zest of ½ orange, cut in fine julienne

4½ tablespoons granulated sugar

2 cups fresh cranberries

5 tablespoons dry white wine

2 tablespoons Grand Marnier

PUMPKIN FILLING

4 tablespoons unsalted butter

4½ tablespoons granulated sugar

I teaspoon ground cinnamon

1½ cups pumpkin puree

APPLE FILLING

2 medium-size apples

4 tablespoons unsalted butter

4½ tablespoons granulated sugar

I tablespoon apple brandy

2 tablespoons heavy cream

Raspberry Puree (page 194) and sweetened whipped cream, for garnish

1. To make the pastry, combine the flour, confectioners' sugar, salt, and 7 tablespoons butter in the bowl of a food processor. Pulse with on/off turns until the mixture is the size of peas. With the processor running, gradually add the eggs, processing just until the dough pulls away from the side of the bowl and forms a ball. Wrap and refrigerate for several hours.

2. To make the cranberry filling, melt 2 tablespoons butter in a heavy medium-size saucepan. Add the orange zest and 4½ tablespoons sugar. Cook over low heat for 10 minutes, stirring occasionally, until the zest is tender. Stir in the cranberries, wine, and Grand Marnier.

3. Bring to a boil. Reduce the heat and boil gently until the berries are tender, 8 to 10 minutes. Cool.

4. To make the pumpkin filling, melt 4 tablespoons butter in a medium-size saucepan. Stir in 4½ tablespoons sugar and the cinnamon until blended. Stir in the pumpkin and mix well.

5. To make the apple filling, peel and core the apples. Using a melon baller, cut them into shapes the size of olives.

6. In a medium-size skillet, melt 4 tablespoons butter over medium

heat. Stir in 4½ tablespoons sugar. Cook until the mixture turns a caramel color, stirring constantly. (It will appear lumpy.)

7. Add the apples. Cook, stirring gently, until almost tender, 2 to 3 minutes. Stir in the brandy, then the cream. Mix gently. Cool.

8. Preheat the oven to 375°F.

9. On a well-floured surface, roll out half the pastry at a time until it is very thin. Cut it to fit tiny shallow tartlet pans or barquette molds.

Press gently into the pans and trim the edges. Prick the dough all over with a fork. Place the pans on a baking sheet.

10. Bake for 6 to 8 minutes, until lightly browned, repricking the pastry if necessary to prevent puffing. Cool in the pans on a rack. Gently remove.

11. Spoon fruit fillings into the cooled tart shells.

12. Serve with raspberry puree and sweetened whipped cream.

$\mathcal{T}$ARTE $\mathcal{T}$ATIN

SERVES 6

This apple pie, made famous by two French sisters named Tatin, is created by covering apples with a puff pastry crust and flipping the finished product after baking so that the crust is on the bottom.

½ (17¼-ounce) package frozen puff pastry (1 sheet)

4 tablespoons unsalted butter

4 Golden Delicious apples, peeled, cored, and thinly sliced

1½ cups sugar

Purple Basil Ice Cream (page 95)

Purple basil sprigs, for garnish

1. Thaw the pastry sheet at room temperature for 20 minutes. In a heavy 9-inch ovenproof skillet, melt the butter over medium-high heat until hot. Add the apples and sprinkle with the sugar. Toss the apples until the sugar dissolves. Cook them, stirring gently, until the sugar caramelizes, 20 to 25 minutes.

2. Preheat the oven to 350°F.

3. Unfold the pastry sheet on a floured surface. Press any seams together to seal. Roll out to a thick-

ness of ⅛ inch. Cut the pastry in a circle the same diameter as the top of the skillet. Fit the pastry over the apples in the skillet.

4. Place the skillet on a baking sheet and bake for 20 to 25 minutes, until the pastry is puffed and turns golden brown.

5. Immediately invert the tart onto a serving dish. Serve it warm with purple basil ice cream and garnish with purple basil sprigs.

Nectarine Tart

SERVES 6

Almond Tart Shell

½ cup slivered almonds

I cup all-purpose flour

¼ cup sugar

3 spiral pieces orange zest

I teaspoon ground mace

10 tablespoons (I¼ sticks) cold
  unsalted butter, cut up

I egg

Nectarine Filling

I¾ pounds nectarines, halved,
  pitted, and, if desired, peeled

⅓ cup sugar

3 tablespoons unsalted butter

2 tablespoons orange liqueur

Glaze

½ cup peach preserves, pressed
  through a sieve

2 tablespoons orange liqueur

Fresh raspberries, for garnish

1. To make the shell, process the almonds to a fine powder in the bowl of a food processor. Add the flour, ¼ cup sugar, the orange zest, and the mace. Process until the zest is in fine pieces. Add 10 tablespoons butter. Pulse with on/off turns until the mixture is evenly crumbly.

2. Add the egg. Process until the dough pulls away from the side of the bowl and forms a ball. Shape the dough into a disk. Wrap and refrigerate for I hour.

3. Flour the top and bottom of the dough and roll it out between two sheets of floured waxed paper. Remove the top sheet of waxed paper and invert the pastry over a 9-inch tart pan with a removable bottom. Carefully peel off the second sheet of waxed paper. The pastry is delicate and tears easily, but it is readily mended by patching and pressing the pieces together with your fingers. Trim the dough even with the edge of the pan.

4. Place the tart pan on a baking sheet. Freeze while preparing the nectarines.

5. Preheat the oven to 400°F.

6. To make the filling, thinly slice the nectarine halves almost through, keeping the halves intact. Fan the sliced halves out in a pinwheel design in the pastry shell.

7. Sprinkle the nectarines with ⅓ cup sugar. Dot with 3 tablespoons butter. Drizzle with 2 tablespoons orange liqueur.

8. Bake the tart on the baking sheet for 50 to 60 minutes, until the sugar caramelizes and the juices bubble in the center of the tart.

9. Cool the tart on a rack for 20 minutes before glazing.

10. While the tart is cooling, make the glaze, mixing together the preserves and 2 tablespoons orange liqueur. Spoon the glaze evenly over nectarines while they are still warm. Garnish with raspberries.

FRANGIPANE LEMON TART

An especially lovely way to serve this tart ~ and to call to mind the joys of spring ~ is to place it on a large glass serving plate and surround it with pesticide-free lemon geranium leaves. Some violets scattered among the leaves and placed on the lemon slices in the center of the tart add just the right final touch.

PASTRY

1½ cups all-purpose flour

3 tablespoons sugar

2 teaspoons grated lemon zest

½ teaspoon salt

½ cup (1 stick) unsalted butter, cut in 8 pieces

1 egg, lightly beaten

FRANGIPANE FILLING

½ cup (1 stick) unsalted butter, softened

1 (8-ounce) package almond paste, kneaded until soft

2 eggs, beaten

1 teaspoon grated lemon zest

½ teaspoon almond extract

1 tablespoon all-purpose flour

GLAZED LEMON SLICES

2 lemons, thinly sliced and seeded

1 cup sugar

Sliced almonds, for garnish

1. To make the pastry, blend 1½ cups flour, 3 tablespoons sugar, 2 teaspoons lemon zest, the salt, and ½ cup butter in the bowl of a food processor until the mixture is the consistency of coarse meal. Pour the mixture into a bowl.

2. With a fork, blend in 1 egg until the dough is moistened and starts to hold together. On a floured surface, knead the dough lightly with your fingertips until it forms a ball. Add a sprinkling of ice water if necessary to form the ball. Wrap the dough and refrigerate for at least 1 hour.

3. Roll out the chilled dough between sheets of floured waxed paper. Carefully peel away the waxed paper and fit the pastry into a 9-inch tart pan. Trim the dough even with the edge of the pan and refrigerate until ready to bake.

4. To make the filling, cream ½ cup butter in the bowl of a food processor. Add the almond paste in small pieces alternately with the 2 beaten eggs. Process until smooth, scraping the side of the bowl often.

5. Add 1 teaspoon zest, the almond extract, and 1 tablespoon flour. Process until blended.

6. Preheat the oven to 350°F.

7. Spread the filling evenly in the bottom of the pastry shell. Bake the tart on a baking sheet for 50 minutes, or until the filling is golden and set. Cool on a rack.

8. While the tart is baking, glaze the lemon slices. Put them in a medium-size saucepan, add enough water to cover, and bring to a boil.

9. Reduce the heat and boil gently until the lemon rinds are tender, 25 to 30 minutes. Remove the slices with a slotted spoon, reserving 1 cup of cooking liquid in the pan. Drain the slices on paper towels.

10. Gradually add 1 cup sugar to the reserved liquid, stirring over medium-low heat until the sugar dissolves completely.

11. Bring to a rapid boil and boil until the liquid becomes a thick syrup. (A small spoonful of syrup should hold its shape when dropped onto a cold saucer.) Remove the syrup from the heat.

12. To serve, arrange the lemon slices in circles on top of the tart. Glaze with some of the hot lemon syrup. Garnish with the sliced almonds.

PEACH PIE

SERVES 6

PASTRY

3 cups all-purpose flour

1½ cups confectioners' sugar

¼ teaspoon salt

1½ cups (3 sticks) unsalted butter, cut up and softened

PEACH FILLING

½ cup granulated sugar

¼ cup all-purpose flour

1 teaspoon ground cardamom

¼ cup lemon juice

6 to 8 peaches

1. Make the pastry in two batches. In the bowl of a food processor, combine 1½ cups flour, ¾ cup confectioners' sugar, and ⅛ teaspoon salt. Process until blended. Add ¾ cup butter. Process with on/off turns until the mixture resembles coarse meal. Process until the dough pulls away from the bowl and forms a ball.

2. Make the second batch of pastry with the remaining flour, sugar, salt, and butter in the same way.

3. Wrap each ball of dough in plastic wrap. Refrigerate for 1 hour.

4. To make the filling, combine the granulated sugar, ¼ cup flour, and the cardamom in a small bowl. Mix well. Stir in the lemon juice. Peel and cube 4 cups of peaches and place them in a large bowl. Gently stir in the sugar mixture.

5. Preheat the oven to 375°F.

6. Roll half the pastry on a well-floured surface to fit into a 9-inch pie plate with enough pastry to flute the edge. Spoon the filling into the pastry shell.

7. Roll out the remaining pastry to an 11-inch circle. Cut it into 1-inch strips. Arrange the strips a half-inch apart in a crisscross pattern on the pie to form a lattice. Flute the edge to seal.

8. Bake the pie on a baking sheet for 55 to 65 minutes, until the filling is bubbling and the crust is golden brown. If the edge of the crust begins to get too brown, cover it with foil. Cool the pie on a rack.

RASPBERRY-PLUM PIE

SERVES 6

PASTRY

2½ cups all-purpose flour, plus
    additional for coating butter

½ cup sugar

14 tablespoons (1¾ sticks) cold
    unsalted butter

2 teaspoons grated lemon zest

2 eggs

RASPBERRY-PLUM FILLING

1 cup sugar

½ cup all-purpose flour

1 teaspoon ground cinnamon

⅛ teaspoon ground nutmeg

1 pound plums, pitted and
    sliced (about 3 cups)

3 half-pints raspberries
    (about 4½ cups)

1 tablespoon unsalted butter

1 egg, for glaze

1. To make the pastry, combine 2½ cups flour and the ½ cup sugar in bowl of a food processor. Pulse on/off twice.

2. Roll the 14 tablespoons butter in the additional flour, then cut it into slices. Roll the slices in flour, then cut into sticks, and then into cubes.

3. Sprinkle the cubes and lemon zest into the flour mixture. Process briefly until the mixture resembles fine meal. While the processor is running, add the 2 eggs. Process just until the eggs are folded in.

4. Knead the dough gently on a floured surface until the pastry forms a ball. Wrap it in plastic wrap and refrigerate for at least 1 hour or up to 3 days.

5. On a floured surface, roll out half the pastry to an 11-inch circle. Carefully fit the pastry into a 9-inch pie plate, leaving ½ to 1 inch overhang all around.

6. Roll out the remaining pastry to a 12-inch circle and place it on a baking sheet. Refrigerate both pastries while you make the filling.

7. Preheat the oven to 375°F.

8. To make the filling, mix together the 1 cup sugar, the ½ cup flour, the cinnamon, and the nutmeg in a small bowl.

9. Put the plums in a large bowl, sprinkle the sugar mixture over the plums. Toss until the plums are thoroughly coated. Add the raspberries and toss together.

10. Spoon the fruit mixture into the pie shell and dot with 1 tablespoon butter.

11. In a small bowl, whisk the egg with 1 tablespoon water.

12. Brush the egg glaze over the edge of the pastry in the pie plate. Drape the pastry circle over the filling. Trim the crust evenly, then tuck the edges under and crimp.

13. Using a small sharp knife or scissors, cut small vents in the upper crust. (Cutting a small plum shape is a nice touch.) Brush the pastry with the remaining egg glaze.

14. Place the pie on a baking sheet to catch any dripping juices. Bake for 50 to 55 minutes, until the juices inside are bubbling near the center of the pie and the crust is a deep golden color.

15. Cool the pie on a rack.

Apple, Cranberry & Blue Cheese Strudel

SERVES 12

Dried cherries, which have a bit of a different texture and are less tart, make an appealing alternative to the cranberries in this strudel.

APPLE CRANBERRY FILLING

5 cups cored, peeled, sliced cooking apples

¾ cup dried cranberries

¾ cup fresh fine white bread crumbs

2 ounces mild blue cheese, such as Danish blue, crumbled

PASTRY

½ cup (1 stick) plus 3 tablespoons unsalted butter

½ pound (10 to 12 sheets) phyllo pastry, thawed if frozen

6 tablespoons fresh fine white bread crumbs

1. To make the filling, mix together the apples, dried cranberries, ¾ cup bread crumbs, and the blue cheese in a large bowl.

2. Preheat the oven to 375°F. Butter a baking sheet.

3. To make the pastry, melt ½ cup of the butter. Gently unroll the phyllo pastry and cover it with a damp tea towel.

4. Spread out a sheet of waxed paper large enough to fit a sheet of the phyllo pastry, which measures 18 by 14 inches. Brush the paper with some of the melted butter.

5. Stack 2 sheets of phyllo pastry on the waxed paper. Brush lightly with butter and sprinkle with 2 tablespoons of the bread crumbs. Layer 1 sheet of phyllo pastry on top and butter it. Layer a fourth sheet, brush it with butter, and sprinkle with 2 tablespoons of the bread crumbs. Continue in this manner on all but 1 sheet of phyllo pastry.

6. Cut the stack of pastry sheets in half to make two stacks that measure 14 by 9 inches each.

7. On each stack, spread half the apple cranberry filling in a 4-inch strip along one long side, leaving a 1-inch border of pastry on three sides. Dot each strip of filling with 1½ tablespoons butter.

8. Cut the reserved pastry sheet in half crosswise and place one half over each strip of filling. Brush with melted butter. Fold in the ends of the stack about 1 inch. Roll the stack loosely, starting at the long side and using the waxed paper to facilitate rolling.

9. Place the strudel seam side down on the prepared baking sheet. Brush the strudel with melted butter.

10. Bake the strudel for 35 minutes, or until golden, brushing it with melted butter several times.

11. Cool the strudel to room temperature on the baking sheet. Cut slices on the diagonal.

NOTE: To make ahead, bake and cool the strudel, wrap it in plastic wrap, and freeze. To serve, bake the frozen strudel for 45 minutes in an oven preheated to 375°F.

Lemon Geranium Pound Cake

SERVES 12 TO 16

Because lemon geranium sprigs are in the bottom of the pan during baking, the flavoring in this pound cake is particularly subtle. The sprigs are removed before the cake is served.

6 pesticide-free lemon geranium sprigs

1½ cups all-purpose flour

1½ cups sugar

¼ teaspoon baking soda

1 cup (2 sticks) unsalted butter, softened and cut in small pieces

Grated zest of 1 lemon

1½ tablespoons lemon juice

1½ teaspoons vanilla extract

5 eggs, separated and at room temperature

⅛ teaspoon salt

1 teaspoon cream of tartar

Strawberries and confectioners' sugar, for garnish

1. Butter and flour a 10-inch tube pan with a removable bottom. Space the lemon geranium sprigs evenly in the bottom of the pan. Preheat the oven to 325°F.

2. Sift the flour, ¾ cup of the sugar, and the baking soda into the large bowl of an electric mixer. Knead in the butter with your fingers until it is blended. Stir in the zest, lemon juice, and vanilla.

3. Beat in the egg yolks, one at a time, at medium speed until blended.

4. In a large bowl, using clean beaters, beat the egg whites and salt at high speed until soft peaks form. Gradually add the remaining ¾ cup sugar, beating until stiff, glossy peaks form, scraping the side of the bowl often.

5. Sift the cream of tartar over the egg whites, then gently fold it into them. Stir several large spoonfuls of egg white into the flour mixture. Fold the remaining egg whites into the flour mixture in three additions.

6. Pour the batter into the prepared pan, gently smoothing the top. Lightly tap the pan on the counter to remove any air bubbles.

7. Bake the cake on a baking sheet for 1 hour, until a cake tester inserted in the center comes out clean. Cool in the pan set on a rack for 10 minutes. Remove the cake from the pan and cool completely on a wire rack.

8. To serve, remove the herb sprigs from the cake. Sift confectioners' sugar over the cake and decorate with sprigs of lemon geranium. Serve with strawberries dipped in confectioners' sugar.

LOVELY IN LACE

A simple but graceful way to make a plain cake something extraordinary is to top it with confectioners' sugar lace. Just place a doily or other template on the surface of the cake and sprinkle on confectioners' sugar through a fine sieve. Then carefully pick the doily straight up. Be sure the cake has cooled to prevent the heat from melting the sugar.

NASTURTIUMS

Lively in the garden and on the tongue, nasturtiums enliven everything with a peppery accent. The leaves can substitute for watercress, and the flowers are so pretty ~ ranging from pale yellow to mahogany ~ you'll want to take every opportunity to use them. Try them for cake decorations and in tea sandwiches mixed with butter or mayonnaise.

STRAWBERRY CREAM CAKE WITH NASTURTIUMS

SERVES 12

CAKE

3 cups cake flour

5 teaspoons baking powder

½ teaspoon salt

1 cup (2 sticks) unsalted butter, softened

2 cups granulated sugar

4 eggs

1 teaspoon vanilla extract

1¼ cups milk

CREAM FILLING

⅓ cup granulated sugar

2 tablespoons cornstarch

2 egg yolks

1½ cups milk

2 teaspoons vanilla extract

WHIPPED CREAM FROSTING

1½ cups heavy cream

1 teaspoon vanilla extract

3 tablespoons confectioners' sugar

1 cup sliced fresh strawberries

Pesticide-free nasturtium blossoms, for garnish

1. To make the cake, generously butter and flour two deep 9 by 2-inch cake pans. Preheat the oven to 350°F.
2. Sift the cake flour, baking powder, and salt into a large bowl.
3. In the large bowl of an electric mixer, cream the butter at medium speed. Gradually add 2 cups granulated sugar, beating until the mixture is light and fluffy. Scrape the side of the bowl often.
4. Add the eggs, one at a time, beating well after each addition. Beat in 1 teaspoon vanilla.
5. Add 1¼ cups milk alternately with the flour mixture, beating until blended after each addition. Spread the batter evenly in the prepared pans.
6. Bake for 40 to 45 minutes, until a cake tester inserted in the center comes out clean. Cool the cakes in the pans set on racks for 10 minutes. Remove the cakes from the pans and cool completely on racks.
7. To make the cream filling, combine ⅓ cup granulated sugar with the cornstarch in a heavy medium-size saucepan. Mix until blended.
8. In a small bowl, whisk together the egg yolks and 1½ cups milk. Whisk that into the sugar mixture. Cook over medium heat, stirring constantly, until the mixture thickens and boils. Cook and stir 1 minute longer.
9. Remove the filling from the heat. Stir in 2 teaspoons vanilla. Pour the filling into a bowl. Press plastic wrap directly on the surface of the filling. Cool to room temperature, about 3 hours.
10. To make the whipped cream frosting, beat the cream with 1 teaspoon vanilla in a chilled bowl at high speed until the cream begins to hold its shape. Gradually add the confectioners' sugar, beating the cream to stiff peaks.
11. To assemble the cake, place one layer on a serving plate. Spread the filling on top, leaving a 1-inch border around the edge of the cake. Arrange the sliced straw-

berries in a single layer over the filling. Place the second layer of cake on the strawberries. Spread the frosting on the top and side of the cake. Refrigerate the cake until serving time. Garnish with the nasturtium blossoms. The cake is best the day it is made.

Wensleydale Apple Cake

SERVES 10

Dolores Snyder, a Texan who has lived in England, shares that country's love of cheese and cooks with it at every opportunity. This traditional apple cake, enhanced with Wensleydale or cheddar cheese, is typical of her cooking.

Apple Cake

2 cups all-purpose flour

1½ teaspoons baking powder

¼ teaspoon salt

½ cup granulated sugar

½ cup (1 stick) unsalted butter, cut up

1 large cooking apple, peeled, cored, and shredded (½ cup)

1 egg

¼ cup milk

Topping

½ cup shredded Wensleydale or white cheddar cheese

1 large cooking apple, peeled, cored, thinly sliced, and brushed with lemon juice to prevent browning

2 tablespoons packed light brown sugar

½ teaspoon ground cinnamon

Whipped cream, for garnish

1. To make the cake, preheat the oven to 350°F. Butter an 8-inch springform pan. Line the bottom of the pan with parchment or waxed paper. Butter the paper.
2. Sift the flour, baking powder, salt, and granulated sugar into a large bowl. With a pastry blender or two knives, cut in ½ cup butter until the mixture resembles fine meal. Toss in the shredded apple.
3. Whisk together the egg and milk. Stir the egg mixture into the apple mixture until blended. The batter will be fairly stiff. Spread the batter evenly in the prepared pan.
4. To make the topping, sprinkle the cheese over the cake. Arrange the apple slices overlapping in pinwheel fashion over the cheese.
5. Mix the brown sugar and cinnamon and sprinkle over the apples.
6. Bake the cake on a baking sheet for 60 to 70 minutes, until a cake tester inserted in the center comes out clean and the center of the cake is puffed and dry.
7. Cool the cake in the pan on a rack for 10 minutes. Loosen the cake with a knife and remove the side of the pan. Cool the cake on a rack.
8. Remove the bottom of the pan and peel off the paper. To serve, cut the cake in wedges and serve with a dollop of whipped cream. The cake is best the day it is made.

APPLES

No food embodies the taste of fall more than the apple, in all its hundreds of splendid personalities ~ Granny Smiths, Golden Delicious, McIntosh, Winesaps, Mutsus, and Northern Spys, just for starters. To go beyond supermarket choices, search out farmers' markets and orchards, especially those that have made a point of helping to preserve varieties that might otherwise disappear.

BROWNIE TORTE

SERVES 8

1 tablespoon fine, dry bread crumbs

2 tablespoons unsweetened cocoa powder

1 cup finely ground blanched almonds

6 tablespoons sifted all-purpose flour

¼ teaspoon salt

½ cup (1 stick) unsalted butter, softened

1⅓ cups granulated sugar

3 eggs, separated

3 ounces unsweetened chocolate, melted and cooled

1 teaspoon vanilla extract

Confectioners' sugar, for garnish

Pesticide-free edible blossoms and leaves, for garnish

1. Preheat the oven to 325°F. Butter a 9-inch springform pan. In a small bowl, mix together the bread crumbs and 1 tablespoon of the cocoa. Coat the bottom of the pan and halfway up the side with the crumb mixture, tapping out any excess.

2. In a medium-size bowl, combine the almonds, flour, the remaining 1 tablespoon of the cocoa, and salt. Mix the ingredients until blended.

3. In the small bowl of an electric mixer, cream the butter and granulated sugar at medium speed until they are light and fluffy. Add the egg yolks, one at a time, beating well after each addition.

4. Beat in the melted chocolate and the vanilla until blended. Gradually fold in the almond mixture.

5. Using clean beaters, beat the egg whites at high speed until stiff peaks form. Gradually fold the egg whites into the chocolate mixture. Gently spread the batter evenly in the prepared pan.

6. Bake the torte on a baking sheet in the lower third of the oven for 35 to 40 minutes, until a cake tester inserted in the center comes out clean. Cool the torte on a rack for 5 minutes.

7. Run a knife around the edge of the torte to loosen it. Remove the side of the pan, then cool the torte completely.

8. Place a 9-inch doily over the top of the cooled torte. Sift the confectioners' sugar over the top of the torte. Lift the doily straight up. The torte can be served on a glass plate, decorated with blossoms and leaves.

Marzipan Butter Cake

CAKE BRUSHING

When you make a layer cake, you'll get a sleeker, more professional-looking finished dessert if you remove any loose crumbs from the layers. It's an especially important step if you're using a glaze and want a smooth sheen. Just take a dry pastry brush and gently sweep the cake all over until it is clean of loose crumbs. Then ice the cake or cover it with filling as desired.

BUTTER CAKE

2½ cups cake flour

1½ cups granulated sugar

1 tablespoon baking powder

1 teaspoon salt

2 tablespoons kirsch

Milk

½ cup (1 stick) unsalted butter, softened

½ teaspoon orange extract

2 eggs

FILLING

1½ cups heavy cream

½ cup superfine sugar

2 tablespoons kirsch

⅓ cup finely chopped candied orange peel

TOPPING

1 (7-ounce) roll marzipan

¼ cup sifted confectioners' sugar, plus additional for garnish

Pesticide-free stephanotis flowers, for garnish

Gold ribbon, silver-coated almonds, candied orange peel, and white chocolate curls, for garnish

1. To make the cake, preheat the oven to 350°F. Butter and flour two 9-inch layer cake pans. Line the bottoms with waxed paper rounds, then butter and flour the paper.

2. Sift together the cake flour, granulated sugar, baking powder, and salt. In a measuring cup, combine the 2 tablespoons kirsch and enough milk to make 1 cup.

3. In the large bowl of an electric mixer, beat the butter at low speed to soften. Add the sifted dry ingredients, ¾ cup of the milk mixture, and the orange extract. Beat at low speed until moistened. Beat at medium speed for 3 minutes, scraping the bowl often.

4. Add the eggs and remaining milk mixture to the batter. Beat at medium speed for 1 minute.

5. Pour the batter into the prepared pans. Bake for 25 to 30 minutes, or until a cake tester inserted in the center comes out clean.

6. Cool the cakes for 10 minutes, then remove them from the pans and cool them completely on racks.

7. To make the filling, whip the heavy cream until it begins to thicken. Gradually add the superfine sugar, then 2 tablespoons kirsch. Beat until stiff peaks form.

8. Reserve two thirds of the whipped cream mixture (about 2 cups). Stir the candied orange peel into the remaining whipped cream.

9. To make the topping, combine the marzipan and ¼ cup confectioners' sugar in the bowl of a food processor. Process until the mixture pulls away from the side of the bowl and forms a ball.

10. Dust two sheets of waxed paper with additional confectioners' sugar.

Roll out the almond mixture between the waxed paper to a little larger than a 10-inch circle. Use a 10-inch plate or 10-inch cake pan to cut the almond mixture into a 10-inch circle.

11. Place one cake layer on a serving plate. Reserve one-third cup of whipped cream with orange peel for garnish and spread the remainder on the cake layer. Place the second layer on the whipped cream.

12. Spread the plain whipped cream generously on the side of the cake and in a thin layer on the top of the cake.

13. Drape the marzipan over the cake in gentle folds. Sift confectioners' sugar on top.

14. Garnish the center of the cake with the reserved whipped cream-candied orange peel mixture and a small cluster of stephanotis tied with gold ribbon. Decorate the top edge of the cake with almonds, peel, and white chocolate curls.

Vanilla Pistachio Nut Cake

SERVES 16

3 cups cake flour
4 teaspoons baking powder
½ teaspoon salt
1 cup (2 sticks) unsalted butter
2 cups sugar
1 cup milk
1 teaspoon vanilla extract
¼ teaspoon almond extract
6 egg whites
½ cup ground natural unsalted pistachio nuts

1. Butter and flour a 12-cup fluted tube pan. Preheat the oven to 350°F.
2. Sift together the flour, baking powder, and salt into a large bowl.
3. In the large bowl of an electric mixer, cream the butter and sugar at medium speed until light and fluffy, scraping the side of the bowl often. Beat in the milk, vanilla, and almond extract alternately with the dry ingredients.
4. In the small bowl of an electric mixer, using clean beaters, beat the egg whites at high speed until stiff peaks form. Gently fold them into the batter. Quickly fold in the ground pistachio nuts.
5. Spread the batter evenly in the prepared pan. Bake for 50 to 60 minutes, until a cake tester inserted in the center of the cake comes out clean. Cool on a rack for 10 minutes. Remove the cake from the pan and cool completely on a rack.

TO FINISH A MEAL

Late-harvest grapes, allowed to linger on the vine and shrivel, are used for dessert wines, an especially satisfying way to end a meal. Among the classics are Château d'Yquem of France and Hungary's Tokay Anzu, but there are many choices, including some from California. Don't serve a dessert wine with a sweet dessert; instead, pair it with a wedge of blue cheese, or let it stand on its own, served very cold.

89

$\mathcal{F}$RAMBOISE $\mathcal{C}$HEESECAKE

SERVES 10

$\mathcal{D}$avid Wood has relished raspberries since he was a boy yearning for the sweet weeks of July, when the berry season converged with summer vacation. Now proprietor of three Toronto gourmet shops, he indulges his longtime love in this recipe.

CRUST

1 cup all-purpose flour, plus additional for coating butter

¼ cup sugar

½ cup (1 stick) cold unsalted butter

RASPBERRY CREAM FILLING

2 (8-ounce) packages cream cheese, softened

¾ cup sugar

2 eggs, plus 1 egg yolk

2 tablespoons framboise liqueur

1 cup Raspberry Puree (page 194)

Crème Fraîche (page 187) or sour cream, for garnish

Fresh raspberries, for garnish

Grated zest of 1 lemon, for garnish

1. Preheat the oven to 350°F. Butter an 8-inch springform pan.

2. To make the crust, put 1 cup flour and ¼ cup sugar in the bowl of a food processor and pulse on/off several times to mix.

3. Roll the butter in the additional flour, then cube it. Drop the butter cubes over the flour mixture in the processor bowl. Process until the mixture resembles coarse meal.

4. Press the dough into the bottom of the prepared pan.

5. To make the filling, beat the cream cheese and ¾ cup sugar in the large bowl of an electric mixer at medium speed until smooth. Beat in the eggs, egg yolk, and framboise liqueur at low speed until blended. Stir in ⅔ cup of the raspberry puree.

6. Pour the cheese mixture into the crust. Carefully pour the remaining raspberry puree in a spiral pattern on top of the filling. Place the pan on a baking sheet .

7. Bake for 45 to 50 minutes, until the edge of the cheesecake pulls away from the pan and the center of the cheesecake is almost set. It will jiggle a little.

8. Remove the cheesecake from the oven and cool completely on a rack, then refrigerate overnight.

9. To serve, run a knife around the edge of the pan to loosen the cheesecake. Remove the side of the pan. Serve each slice of cheesecake with a small dollop of crème fraîche. Drop a few raspberries into the crème fraîche and top with a sprinkling of the zest.

MARBLED PUMPKIN CHEESECAKE

SERVES 12 TO 16

"What calls back the past, like the rich pumpkin pie?" asked poet John Greenleaf Whittier. This dessert combines the memories that pumpkin pie may conjure up with the luxury of cheesecake. It's a winning combination.

GRAHAM CRACKER CRUST

1¼ cups graham cracker crumbs

2 tablespoons granulated sugar

4 tablespoons unsalted butter, melted

1 cup miniature semisweet chocolate pieces

PUMPKIN CHEESECAKE

1 cup miniature semisweet chocolate pieces

3 (8-ounce) packages cream cheese, softened

1 cup granulated sugar

¼ cup packed light brown sugar

1 (16-ounce) can pumpkin puree

4 eggs

½ cup canned evaporated milk

¼ cup cornstarch

¾ teaspoon ground cinnamon

⅛ teaspoon ground nutmeg

1. To make the crust, butter a 10-inch springform pan. Mix together the graham cracker crumbs, 2 tablespoons granulated sugar, and the butter. Press the mixture evenly on the bottom of the pan. Sprinkle the crust with 1 cup chocolate pieces.

2. Preheat the oven to 325°F.

3. To make the cheesecake, melt 1 cup chocolate pieces in a heavy small saucepan over low heat, stirring constantly, until smooth.

4. In the large bowl of an electric mixer, beat the cream cheese, 1 cup granulated sugar, and the brown sugar at medium speed until smooth. Beat in the pumpkin puree. Beat in the eggs and evaporated milk until blended. Sift in the cornstarch, cinnamon, and nutmeg. Beat just until mixed.

5. Stir 1 cup of the pumpkin mixture into the melted chocolate. Mix until evenly blended.

6. Pour the remaining pumpkin filling into the crust. Spoon the chocolate mixture on top of the filling in small mounds. Swirl the chocolate into the pumpkin with a knife. Place the springform pan on a baking sheet.

7. Bake for 60 minutes, or until the edge of the filling is set. The center will jiggle. Turn off the heat and let the cheesecake stand in the oven with the door closed for 30 minutes. Remove the cheesecake to a rack and cool to room temperature, about 3 hours.

8. Cover the cheesecake and refrigerate for several hours before serving.

CHOCOLATE-DIPPED STRAWBERRIES

MAKES 12 TO 16

12 to 16 large strawberries
with stems

4 ounces German sweet
chocolate, broken up

¼ cup sugar

¼ cup heavy cream

2 tablespoons unsalted butter

½ teaspoon vanilla extract

1. Wash the strawberries and pat thoroughly dry on paper towels. Line a baking sheet with parchment or waxed paper.

2. In the top of a double boiler over simmering water, stir the chocolate, sugar, cream, butter, and vanilla until the chocolate is melted and the mixture is smooth. Remove the pan from the heat, but leave the chocolate over the hot water in the double boiler.

3. Working quickly, dip the strawberries in the chocolate, swirling until coated. Hold them over the chocolate until any excess drips off.

4. Arrange the strawberries on the baking sheet. Refrigerate them until ready to serve.

PEACHY SUMMER COOLER

SERVES 5

2 cups peeled, chopped
peaches

1 cup sugar

½ cup lemon juice

6 cups peach ice cream

1⅔ cups cold peach carbonated
beverage

Whipped cream, for garnish

1. Chill 5 ice cream soda glasses.

2. In a medium-size saucepan, combine the peaches and sugar with 2 cups water. Mix well. Bring to a boil over medium heat, stirring often. Reduce the heat and boil gently, stirring often, until the peaches are very tender, about 3 minutes. Pour the mixture into a heatproof bowl, cover with plastic wrap, and refrigerate until cool.

3. In the bowl of a food processor, puree half the peach mixture with on/off turns. Pour the puree into a bowl. Repeat with the remaining peach mixture. Stir in the lemon juice. Cover and refrigerate until the mixture is cold.

4. To serve, pour about ¾ cup of the peach puree into each of the chilled glasses. Spoon scoops of ice cream into each. Add ⅓ cup of the sparkling beverage to each glass and stir gently to mix.

5. Garnish with whipped cream.

THE BEE'S GIFT

*H*oney, *known in ancient*
times as the food of
the gods, takes the flavor of
the flowers from which
the nectar comes. To tailor
any honey to your
personal taste, warm it
on the stove with a flavoring
~ berries, lavender, or
ginger, among others ~
before using.

HONEY ICE CREAM

MAKES 5 1/2 CUPS

2 cups milk
2 cups heavy cream
¾ cup flavored honey

6 egg yolks
¼ cup sugar

1. In a heavy large saucepan, warm the milk, 1 cup of the cream, and the honey over medium-low heat, stirring until the honey dissolves. Cover and keep the mixture warm over low heat.
2. In the small bowl of an electric mixer, beat the egg yolks and sugar at high speed until the mixture turns pale yellow, 5 to 8 minutes. Put the mixture in the large bowl of an electric mixer and very slowly beat in the warm milk mixture at medium speed. Pour the custard back into the saucepan.
3. Cook the custard over medium heat, stirring constantly, until it coats the back of a wooden spoon. Do not allow it to boil.
4. Remove the pan from the heat and pour the custard into a bowl. Mix in the remaining cup of heavy cream. Place the bowl in a larger bowl filled with ice water to chill the custard, stirring occasionally. Make sure the ice water does not spill into the custard.
5. Freeze the mixture in an ice cream machine according to the manufacturer's directions, then cover and freeze for at least 4 hours.

LAVENDER ICE CREAM

MAKES 1 QUART

1 teaspoon dried lavender
   flowers
¾ cup sugar
2 cups milk
⅛ teaspoon salt

4 egg yolks
¼ cup lavender, wildflower, or
   herb honey
1 cup heavy cream

1. Process the flowers and sugar in a food processor until blended.
2. In a medium-size saucepan, scald the milk. Stir in the lavender sugar and salt until dissolved.
3. In the top of a double boiler, whisk the egg yolks until light and smooth. Gradually whisk in the hot milk. Cook the mixture over boiling water, stirring constantly, until it is thick and smooth.
4. Remove the mixture from the heat. Stir in the honey until dissolved. Gradually stir in the cream. Pour the custard into a bowl. Press plastic wrap on the surface and refrigerate for 3 hours.
5. Freeze the mixture in an ice cream machine according to the manufacturer's directions, then cover and freeze for at least 4 hours.

Purple Basil Ice Cream

MAKES ABOUT 5 1/2 CUPS

Etienne Jaulin, chef at the historic Old Angler's Inn in Potomac, Maryland, cultivates the herbs that inspire unusual creations such as this. Purple basil has a spicier flavor than its ubiquitous green cousin; look for it at farmers' markets. Serve this ice cream with Tarte Tatin (page 75).

12 large sprigs purple basil
4 cups milk

8 egg yolks
I cup sugar

1. Bring the basil and milk to a boil in a large saucepan. Remove the pan from the heat, cover, and set aside.
2. In the large bowl of an electric mixer, beat the egg yolks and sugar at high speed until the mixture becomes thick and lemon-colored, about 5 minutes. Scrape the side of the bowl often.
3. Strain the milk, discarding the basil. Gradually beat the hot milk into the egg mixture. Pour the custard into a heavy large saucepan.

Cook over medium heat, stirring constantly, until the mixture thickens and coats the back of a spoon.
4. Strain the custard into a medium-size bowl. Place the bowl in an ice-water bath (page 94) for half an hour, stirring often.
5. Refrigerate until the custard is cold, at least 2½ hours. Pour the custard into an ice cream machine and freeze according to the manufacturer's directions. Cover tightly and freeze for at least 4 hours.

Mixed-Berry Sorbet

MAKES 3 CUPS

I cup sugar
½ cup raspberries
½ cup sliced strawberries

¼ cup blackberries
¼ cup blueberries
¼ cup raspberry liqueur

1. In a small saucepan, bring the sugar and 2 cups of water to a boil, stirring to dissolve the sugar. Refrigerate the syrup until it is cold.
2. In a blender, combine all the berries, the liqueur, and 2 cups of syrup. Blend just until the berries

are pureed. Press the puree through a fine sieve, discarding the pulp.
3. Freeze the sorbet in an ice cream machine according to the manufacturer's directions, then cover and freeze for at least 4 hours.

Menus to Remember

AN ELEGANT DINNER PARTY

A Cordial Invitation

Comforts of the Morning

*B*reakfast is an informal affair, with newspapers being read and people coming and going as school or work demands. But make it brunch, and the tone changes as family and friends settle in for a leisurely meal. Mary F. Henderson, in her 1878 "Practical Cooking and Dinner Giving," suggested that some people prefer breakfast parties because "dinner parties are mere formalities; but you invite a man to breakfast because you want to see him."

GRAPEFRUIT, RASPBERRIES & KIWIFRUITS IN CHAMPAGNE

SERVES 4

Jamie and Jack Davies, who revived the nineteenth-century Schramsberg Vineyard to produce sparkling wines that rival those of France, believe that Champagne is not just for special occasions; the proof is in this spirited yet delicate compote.

3 small grapefruits
½ pint raspberries
1 tablespoon sugar
2 kiwifruits, peeled and sliced

1 cup chilled Champagne
Mint sprigs, for garnish

1. Pare the grapefruits and section them over a bowl to catch the juice. Add the grapefruit sections to the juice in the bowl. Sieve half the raspberries into the grapefruit. Add the remaining berries. Sprinkle the sugar over the fruit and mix gently. Cover and refrigerate the fruit.

2. Just before serving, gently stir the kiwi slices into the fruit mixture. Slowly pour the chilled Champagne over the fruit and mix gently.
3. Serve the fruit cocktails in sherbet glasses, garnished with mint sprigs, if desired.

HOT CHOCOLATE

Until bar candy was

perfected in the mid-1800's,

the only way to satisfy

a taste for chocolate was by

sipping it hot. But even

with so many bars to choose

from at modern candy

shops, cocoa is a luxurious

choice. And all the more

so when poured from chocolate

pots, which are tall and

slender and sometimes have a

hole in the lid for

whisking up a rich foam.

CRANBERRY PEAR COMPOTE

SERVES 6 TO 8

3 cinnamon spice tea bags
4 large pears, peeled, cored, and halved
1½ cups sugar
1½ cups cranberries
1 whole nutmeg

1 cinnamon stick
2 tablespoons pear brandy
1 tablespoon lemon juice

1. In a large saucepan, bring 4 cups of water to a boil. Add the tea bags and the pears and return to a boil. Reduce the heat, cover, and simmer the mixture until the pears are tender but not mushy, 5 to 15 minutes. Drain and cool.
2. In a medium-size saucepan, bring to a boil 1½ cups of water and the sugar, cranberries, nutmeg, and cinnamon stick. Stir to dissolve the sugar. Boil gently for 1 to 2 minutes, until the cranberries are plump and their skins have just started to pop.
3. Remove the cranberries with a slotted spoon and reserve. Boil the syrup for 5 minutes. Cool.
4. Remove the nutmeg and cinnamon stick from the cooled syrup. Stir in the brandy and lemon juice.
5. In a serving bowl, combine the pears, cranberries, and syrup. Cover and refrigerate until serving time.

POACHED EGGS WITH ASIAGO CHEESE SAUCE

SERVES 4

*W*ell beyond ordinary poached eggs, this dish would make a good main course for a surprise Father's Day breakfast. Asiago is a rich Italian cheese made from cow's milk.

2 tablespoons unsalted butter
2 tablespoons all-purpose flour
½ cup chicken broth
½ cup heavy cream
½ cup (2 ounces) grated Asiago
4 slices sweet Virginia ham

2 English muffins, split, toasted, and buttered
4 eggs
Freshly ground pepper

1. In a small saucepan, melt the butter. Blend in the flour and stir over medium-high heat for 1 minute.

2. Whisk in the chicken broth and cream. Cook, whisking constantly, until the sauce is thickened and bubbly. Whisk in the cheese until melted. Remove from the heat and cover to keep warm.

3. On a baking sheet, arrange the ham slices on English muffin halves.

Broil them 3 inches from the heat for 2 minutes. Keep them warm.

4. In a large skillet, bring ½ inch of water to a boil and reduce the heat. Slip the eggs into the water and simmer for 4 to 6 minutes. Baste the yolks with simmering water. Remove the eggs with a slotted spoon and arrange over the ham.

5. Serve the muffins with the cheese sauce and freshly ground pepper.

OMELET WITH SMOKED HAM & CHEDDAR CHEESE

MAKES 1 OMELET

5 teaspoons unsalted butter
½ cup cubed smoked ham
2 eggs

Salt and pepper to taste
¼ cup shredded cheddar cheese

1. In a small skillet, melt 2 teaspoons of butter and sauté the ham. Keep the ham warm.

2. In a small bowl, whisk the eggs, salt, and pepper vigorously with a fork for about 10 seconds, just enough to thoroughly blend the yolks and whites.

3. Preheat a heavy 8-inch nonstick skillet over high heat. When a drop of water sizzles on the surface, add 2 teaspoons of the remaining butter, tilting the pan to swirl the butter across the bottom and side. Do not let the butter brown. When the foam on the butter starts to subside, add the eggs.

4. Cook the eggs undisturbed for about 5 seconds. Then, using a spatula, pull cooked egg from the

edge of the pan toward the center, allowing liquid egg to run underneath onto the hot pan. Cook about 20 seconds (the eggs should still be moist and creamy).

5. With the spatula, push the omelet to one side of the pan. Sprinkle it with the cheese. Top half the omelet with the ham. With the spatula, fold the unfilled half over the ham.

6. Let the omelet cook for 5 seconds more to brown the bottom lightly. Quickly tilt the pan upside down over a plate so that the omelet falls out bottom side up.

7. Draw the remaining 1 teaspoon of butter over the top of the omelet to make it shiny.

COFFEEPOTS

A hastily gulped cupful each morning does not give coffee its due. How much more satisfying to make it an afternoon ritual, replete with sweet and savory snacks. A turn-of-the-century wedding gift might have been a cut crystal coffeepot. Today, a large silver urn means that guests can fill ~ and refill ~ their cups at their leisure.

THYME

An essential ingredient in the robust cooking of Provence, thyme marries perfectly with fish and is a lovely addition to bouquets garnis, stuffings, stews, and salads. This culinary herb grows in profusion and in many varieties, including lemon, caraway, and nutmeg. Fresh sprigs impart a deep aroma, but even dried thyme holds its flavor. Thyme has long been thought to have curative powers as well; soldiers used it as a battlefield antiseptic in World War I, and today it appears in mouthwashes, toothpastes, and household disinfectants. Herbal expert Emelie Tolley takes a cup of thyme tea, sometimes laced with ginger and sage, to ward off a cold.

Herbed Scrambled Eggs

SERVES 4

This dish is full of the delicate flavors of fresh herbs. Use organic eggs if they are available; you may prefer the taste. Serve these along with seasonal fruit.

I brioche loaf or other rich bread, cut in 8 slices ½ inch thick

½ cup (I stick) unsalted butter

8 slices Canadian bacon, ¼ inch thick

12 eggs

½ cup lightly packed herbs such as basil, chervil, and thyme, chopped

¼ cup sour cream

Herb sprigs, for garnish

Steamed asparagus or broccoli, for garnish

1. Preheat the oven to 250°F.
2. Using a 2½-inch round cookie cutter, cut the bread slices in 8 rounds. Melt 3 tablespoons of the butter in a large nonstick skillet over medium heat. Brown the brioche rounds in butter on both sides. Cook slowly to ensure even browning. Place them on a baking sheet and keep warm in the low-temperature oven. (Do not cover them, or the croutons will become soft.)
3. In the same skillet, over medium heat, melt 2 tablespoons of the butter. Sauté the bacon in the butter for 30 to 60 seconds on each side. Remove the bacon from the skillet and arrange it in a shal-low baking dish; cover the bacon and keep it warm in the oven.
4. Drain the skillet and wipe with a paper towel.
5. In a large bowl, whisk the eggs. Add the chopped herbs and sour cream. Whisk until blended.
6. Melt the remaining 3 table-spoons of butter in the skillet over medium heat. Add the egg mix-ture and cook slowly, stirring constantly with a wooden spoon, until the eggs are softly scrambled.
7. To serve, arrange 2 croutons on each plate. Layer the Canadian bacon slices over the croutons and spoon the eggs on top. Garnish with herb sprigs, and steamed asparagus or broccoli.

Mushroom-Leek Frittata

SERVES 6 TO 8

Connecticut caterer Susan Kochman tempts guests at her own autumn parties with this frittata, rich with wild mushrooms. Use any variety you particularly like, or try a combination of mushrooms you find at your farmers' market.

4 tablespoons unsalted butter

8 ounces assorted fresh wild mushrooms, sliced

1 leek (white portion only), cut in julienne

3 sprigs savory, or 1 teaspoon dried

10 eggs

¼ cup heavy cream

½ teaspoon baking powder

¼ teaspoon salt

Pinch of pepper

Whole wild mushrooms, for garnish

Savory sprigs, for garnish

1. Brush a heavy nonstick 11-inch skillet generously with oil. Melt the butter in the skillet over medium-high heat. Sauté the mushrooms, leek, and savory in the butter until the vegetables are tender and their juices evaporate. Remove the skillet from the heat, remove the savory sprigs, and spread the vegetables evenly over the skillet.

2. In the small bowl of an electric mixer, combine the eggs, cream, baking powder, salt, and pepper. Beat at medium-low speed until the mixture is blended and foamy.

3. Gently pour the egg mixture over the vegetables. Cover the skillet with a tight-fitting lid. Cook over medium heat for 10 to 12 minutes, until the frittata is set on top and in the center.

4. Run a spatula around and underneath the frittata to loosen it. Invert the skillet onto a serving platter. Garnish the frittata with the whole wild mushrooms and the savory sprigs. Cut in wedges to serve.

SAGE

With its silvery leaves and pungent aroma, sage reminds one of nothing more than the Thanksgiving turkey stuffing, where it has admirably held a starring role. Yet, it is a more versatile player, giving a clean taste to sausages and other fatty meats, cheeses, corn bread, or soups. Sage tea is popular in some countries. Beware, it is a powerful herb ~ long ago associated with long life ~ and you may want to use it sparingly.

BACON QUICHE TARTLETS

Sisters Isabelle and Valérie Ganachaud grew up amid the aroma of fresh-baked bread rising from their father's ground-floor bakery, one of Paris's most famous. When he retired, they couldn't bear to see a baking dynasty stretching back four generations disappear. So they left their previous professions and became the only women to have earned the respected diploma of Maître de Boulangerie. Now they preside over La Flûte Gana, where they turn out such favorites as these tartlets.

1⅔ cups all-purpose flour
Pinch of salt
⅔ cup unsalted butter, softened
4 ounces slab bacon, cut in ¼-inch cubes
2 eggs, plus 1 egg white

1 cup milk
½ cup Crème Fraîche (page 187) or sour cream
Salt and pepper to taste

1. In a medium-size bowl, combine the flour and salt. With a pastry blender or two knives, cut in the butter until the mixture resembles fine meal. Sprinkle 4 to 5 tablespoons of ice water over the mixture, a little at a time, tossing with a fork until all is moistened.
2. Gather the dough into a ball and shape it into a flat rectangle. Wrap the dough in plastic wrap and refrigerate for 1 hour.
3. Butter 6 round tartlet molds that measure 4 inches in diameter and are ¾ inch deep.
4. Cut the dough into 6 equal portions. On a floured board, roll out each portion. Trim the dough to 5½-inch circles with a template or lid. Press the dough into the molds. Fold the edges over and

crimp. Let the dough stand uncovered for 45 minutes to dry slightly.
5. Preheat the oven to 375°F.
6. In a medium-size skillet, cook the bacon cubes over medium heat until browned, stirring often. Drain on paper towels.
7. In a medium-size bowl, whisk together the eggs and egg white. Whisk in the milk and crème fraîche, and season with salt and pepper.
8. Arrange the molds on a baking sheet. Sprinkle the bacon cubes on the bottom of the tart shells, then pour the egg mixture over them, filling the molds almost to the top.
9. Bake the tarts for 50 to 60 minutes, until the tops are a deep golden brown. Let them stand 10 minutes, then serve warm.

Pecan Waffles with Spiced Clementine Sauce

SERVES 4

3 clementines, plus ½ cup strained clementine juice

½ cup plus 3 tablespoons sugar

2 tablespoons cornstarch

¾ cup dry white wine

1 (3-inch) cinnamon stick

3 whole cloves

1¾ cups sifted cake flour

2 teaspoons baking powder

½ teaspoon salt

1½ cups milk

¼ cup unsalted butter, melted and cooled

3 eggs, separated

¾ cup chopped toasted pecans

Mint sprigs, for garnish

1. Peel the clementines, removing all the pith and membrane. Separate the clementines into segments.
2. In a small saucepan, combine ½ cup of the sugar and the cornstarch. Mix well. Stir in the wine, clementine juice, cinnamon stick, cloves, and clementine segments. Cook over medium-high heat, stirring constantly, until the mixture thickens and boils.
3. Pour the sauce into a small bowl. Press plastic wrap directly on the surface of the sauce. Cool until warm, about 1 hour.
4. Sift the cake flour, baking powder, salt, and the remaining 3 tablespoons of sugar into a large bowl.

5. In the medium-size bowl of an electric mixer, beat the milk, butter, and egg yolks at medium speed until blended. Whisk the milk mixture into the flour mixture until smooth.
6. Using clean beaters, beat the egg whites at high speed until they form stiff peaks. Fold the egg whites into the batter. Fold in the pecans. The batter will be very thin.
7. Bake the batter in a waffle iron, following the manufacturer's directions, until golden.
8. To serve the waffles, remove the cinnamon stick and cloves from the sauce. Stir the sauce and ladle it over the waffles. Garnish the waffles with mint sprigs.

CUPS & SAUCERS

No need for a matching set of cups and saucers for tea. A lovely alternative is a collection of beautiful old pieces of china. Try matching a cup to a guest's personality, or let your company choose the cup that appeals most.

Honey Waffles

SERVES 5 OR 6

¼ cup honey

2 cups milk

5 tablespoons unsalted butter, melted

2½ cups all-purpose flour

4 teaspoons baking powder

3 eggs, separated

1 teaspoon orange oil, or 2 tablespoons orange blossom water (optional)

Confectioners' sugar and whipped cream, for garnish

Fresh raspberries

Honey Butter (page 186)

1. In a medium-size saucepan, stir the honey and milk over medium heat until the honey dissolves. Stir in the butter. Cool the mixture.

2. Sift the flour and baking powder into the large bowl of an electric mixer. Whisk the egg yolks and orange flavoring, if using, into the cooled milk mixture. Add that to the flour mixture and beat at medium speed just until smooth.

3. Using clean beaters and the small bowl of an electric mixer, beat the egg whites at high speed until they form stiff peaks. Fold the egg whites into the batter.

4. Bake the batter in a waffle iron, following the manufacturer's directions, until golden.

5. Garnish the waffles with a sprinkling of confectioners' sugar and rosettes of whipped cream. Serve them with fresh raspberries and honey butter.

Sage Sausage Patties

MAKES 2 DOZEN 2-INCH PATTIES

1½ pounds ground uncooked turkey (preferably freshly ground)

1½ pounds ground uncooked pork sausage

1 medium-size onion, coarsely chopped

½ cup Italian parsley, finely chopped

2 tablespoons finely chopped fresh sage, or 2 teaspoons dried

6 garlic cloves, finely minced

2 teaspoons ground ginger

2 teaspoons red pepper flakes

1 teaspoon ground cloves

1 teaspoon black pepper

1. In a large mixing bowl, thoroughly combine the turkey and pork sausage, using your fingers or two forks. Add the onion, parsley, sage, garlic, ginger, pepper flakes, ground cloves, and black pepper. Mix well.

2. By hand, form the mixture into 24 patties, each 2 inches in diameter and ¾ to 1 inch thick.

3. Arrange the patties in two very large skillets. Cook them over medium heat for 12 to 17 minutes, until they are cooked through in the center, turning once.

Buckwheat Crêpes with Smoked Salmon

SERVES 6

There's not much more work to making crêpes than to making pancakes, but as this recipe and the one that follows make clear, crêpes are far more elegant. Stacked between sheets of waxed paper and wrapped in plastic wrap, leftover crêpes can be frozen and filled another time.

SMOKED SALMON FILLING

9 ounces thinly sliced smoked salmon

Juice of 1 lemon

1 tablespoon chopped dill

1½ cups sour cream or yogurt

2 tablespoons salmon caviar, for garnish

Dill sprigs, for garnish

BUCKWHEAT CRÊPES

3 eggs

⅔ cup milk

½ cup buckwheat or whole-wheat flour

½ cup all-purpose flour

3 tablespoons unsalted butter, melted and cooled, plus additional for the pan

1. To make the filling, place the salmon slices in a shallow nonreactive dish and sprinkle them with the lemon juice and chopped dill. Cover and refrigerate for 4 hours.

2. To make the crêpes, combine the eggs, ⅔ cup of water, and the milk in the small bowl of an electric mixer. Beat at medium speed until blended. Add the buckwheat flour, the all-purpose flour, and 3 tablespoons of butter. Beat until smooth.

3. Heat a 6-inch crêpe pan or a small skillet over medium-high heat. Brush the pan with melted butter before making each crêpe.

4. Pour about 2 tablespoons of the batter into the prepared pan, tilting it quickly to spread the batter evenly on the bottom and slightly up the side of the pan. Cook quickly on each side. To keep them warm, stack the cooked crêpes on a heated plate covered with a tea towel.

5. To serve, spoon a dollop of sour cream on each warm crêpe. Top the sour cream with slices of salmon. Fold the crêpe around the filling. Top with a spoonful of sour cream, salmon caviar, and dill sprigs.

Crêpes with Berry Filling

SERVES 6

ORANGE SAUCE

3 eggs

½ cup orange juice

½ cup granulated sugar

¼ cup unsalted butter, cut in pieces

I tablespoon grated orange zest

Pinch of salt

2 tablespoons Grand Marnier or Curaçao

BERRY FILLING

2½ cups raspberries, blueberries, or sliced strawberries

2 tablespoons granulated sugar

2 tablespoons Grand Marnier or Curaçao

I teaspoon grated orange zest

CRÊPES

3 eggs

⅔ cup milk

I cup all-purpose flour

3 tablespoons unsalted butter, melted and cooled, plus additional for the pan

Confectioners' sugar and grated orange zest, for garnish

1. To make the sauce, whisk together the 3 eggs, orange juice, ½ cup sugar, ¼ cup butter, I tablespoon orange zest, and salt with ¼ cup of water in the top of a double boiler. Cook over simmering water, stirring constantly, until thickened.

2. Remove the pan from the water and stir in the 2 tablespoons of Grand Marnier. Place plastic wrap directly on the surface of the sauce. Cool, then refrigerate.

3. To make the filling, combine the berries, 2 tablespoons sugar, 2 tablespoons Grand Marnier, and I teaspoon orange zest in a bowl. Mix gently. Cover and refrigerate.

4. To make the crêpes, combine the 3 eggs, ⅔ cup of water, and the milk. Beat at medium speed until blended. Add the flour and melted butter. Beat until smooth.

5. Heat a 6-inch crêpe pan or a small skillet over medium-high heat. Brush the pan with melted butter before making each crêpe.

6. Pour about 2 tablespoons of batter into the prepared pan, tilting it quickly to spread batter evenly on the bottom and slightly up the side. Cook 6 crêpes quickly on each side. Stack the cooked crêpes on a heated plate covered with a tea towel. Leftover batter can be covered and refrigerated up to 24 hours.

7. To serve, spread berry filling on the crêpes. Roll the crêpes up and dust with confectioners' sugar. Spoon orange sauce over the crêpes and sprinkle with orange zest.

Menus to Remember

MOTHER'S DAY BREAKFAST

Amaretti Rhubarb Coffee Cake

SERVES 8 TO 10

Amarettini are miniature versions of the almond-flavored Italian cookies known as amaretti, available at specialty and Italian food shops. They often come in a tin and are wrapped in tissue paper.

COFFEE CAKE

1 teaspoon active dry yeast

½ teaspoon plus 2 tablespoons sugar

3 tablespoons unsalted butter

½ teaspoon vanilla extract or grated orange zest

¼ teaspoon salt

1 egg

¼ cup warm (110°F) milk

1½ cups unbleached all-purpose flour

FRUIT FILLING

2¼ cups thinly sliced fresh rhubarb (about 12 ounces)

½ cup sugar

1 teaspoon ground cinnamon

1 egg yolk

6 tablespoons half-and-half

1 tablespoon almond liqueur

AMARETTI STREUSEL

1 (2.6-ounce) package amarettini cookies (about 60)

¼ cup all-purpose flour

¼ cup sugar

1 teaspoon ground cinnamon or grated orange zest

5 tablespoons cold unsalted butter, cut in small pieces

Thin strips orange zest, for garnish

1. Generously butter a 9 by 9 by 2-inch baking pan.

2. To make the coffee cake, sprinkle the yeast and ½ teaspoon of the sugar over 2 tablespoons of warm water in a small bowl. Stir to dissolve the yeast and let stand until foamy, 5 to 10 minutes.

3. In the small bowl of an electric mixer, cream the 3 tablespoons butter, the remaining 2 tablespoons sugar, the vanilla, and the salt at medium speed until light and fluffy, about 3 minutes. Scrape the side of the bowl often. Beat in the egg, milk, and yeast mixture.

4. Add ½ cup of the flour and beat at medium speed for 3 minutes. Add the remaining flour ¼ cup at a time, beating after each addition. The batter will be sticky and stiff.

5. Spread the batter in the prepared pan, cover it loosely with plastic wrap, and let rise in a warm place until puffy, about 30 minutes.

6. To make the filling, toss the rhubarb in a medium-size bowl with the ½ cup sugar and 1 teaspoon cinnamon.

7. In another bowl, beat the egg yolk, half-and-half, and almond liqueur with a fork until blended.

NAPKIN FOLDING

"There was a row of bouquets all down the table; and on the wide-bordered plates the napkins stood like bishops' mitres, each with an oval-shaped roll between the folds." So wrote Gustave Flaubert in Madame Bovary. *Like every other detail, napkins were attended to with great care. In fact, for special occasions, professional folders were dispatched to create fruit or flowers or crisply folded parcels or fans.*

8. To make the streusel, combine the cookies, ¼ cup flour, ¼ cup sugar, and I teaspoon cinnamon in the bowl of a food processor. Process until the cookies are broken into coarse crumbs. Add the 5 tablespoons butter and process with on/off turns until the mixture forms coarse crumbs.

9. Preheat the oven to 375°F.

10. Combine the fruit and half-and-half mixtures, stirring until the fruit is evenly moistened. Gently spoon over the batter. Sprinkle the fruit evenly with the streusel.

11. Bake the coffee cake for 40 to 45 minutes, until the fruit is tender and the streusel is crisp. Cool.

12. Cut the cake into diamond-shaped pieces. Arrange the cake on a serving platter and garnish with a bow of orange zest strips.

FRUIT & NUT RING WITH GLAZE

SERVES 12

The candied fruit in this cake may make you think of Christmas, but you can make your decorations reflect any occasion ~ slice the cherries to form daisy petals in the warm months, for example, or hearts in February.

FRUIT AND NUT RING	GLAZE
1¾ cups all-purpose flour	⅓ cup kirsch
I teaspoon baking powder	⅓ cup sugar
⅔ cup raisins	
⅔ cup chopped mixed candied fruits	Candied cherries and whole blanched almonds, for garnish
⅓ cup chopped almonds	
1¾ cups (3½ sticks) unsalted butter, softened	
I cup sugar	
3 eggs	

1. To make the ring, butter and flour an 8-cup ring mold. Preheat the oven to 325°F.

2. In a medium-size bowl, combine the flour, baking powder, raisins, chopped candied fruits, and chopped almonds. Mix well.

3. In the large bowl of an electric mixer, beat the butter and I cup sugar at medium speed until fluffy,

about 5 minutes. Add the eggs, I at a time, beating after each. Gradually stir in the flour mixture. Mix thoroughly.

4. Spoon the batter evenly into the prepared mold. Set the mold on a baking sheet and bake for 60 to 70 minutes, until a cake tester inserted in the center comes out clean. (The cake will rise very high.)

5. Cool the cake for 10 minutes in the mold set on a rack. Run a knife around the edge of the mold to loosen the cake. Remove the cake and cool on the rack until warm.

6. Meanwhile, make the glaze: In a small saucepan, bring the kirsch and ⅓ cup sugar to a boil, stirring to dissolve the sugar. Boil gently until the glaze is smooth and slightly thickened, about 5 minutes.

7. Drizzle the warm glaze over the warm cake. Garnish with candied cherries and almonds.

LEMON POPPY MUFFINS

MAKES 30 MUFFINS

3 cups unbleached all-purpose flour

1½ teaspoons baking powder

1½ teaspoons baking soda

½ teaspoon salt

¾ cup unsalted butter, softened

1 cup plus 2 tablespoons sugar, plus additional for garnish

3 eggs

1 cup sour cream

⅓ cup lemon juice

1½ teaspoons vanilla extract

¼ cup poppy seeds

1 teaspoon grated lemon zest

1. Preheat the oven to 375°F. Line 30 muffin cups with paper liners.

2. Sift together the flour, baking powder, baking soda, and salt.

3. Cream the butter and sugar in the large bowl of an electric mixer at medium speed until fluffy, scraping the side of the bowl often. Add the eggs, one at a time, beating well after each addition.

4. Add the flour mixture alternately with the sour cream, lemon juice, and vanilla, beating at low speed until blended. Fold in the poppy seeds and lemon zest.

5. Fill the lined muffin cups two thirds full. Sprinkle the tops with sugar, if desired.

6. Bake for 18 to 20 minutes, until a cake tester inserted in the center comes out clean. Cool the muffins on a rack before serving.

A Fine Respite

*S*ometimes the most generous part of being a hostess is bringing together people who otherwise would not know one another. More than a decade ago, cookbook author Helen Gustafson realized that her wonderful friends, all of whom shared a love of food, did not know one another. Thus was born Helen's tea circle, which has persevered through marriages, births, and moves.

Vanilla Hazelnut Biscotti

MAKES 5 DOZEN

2 eggs, plus 1 egg white
1 tablespoon Vanilla Brandy (page 187)
1 cup Vanilla Sugar (page 70)
Pinch of salt

2¼ cups all-purpose flour
1½ teaspoons baking powder
1 cup coarsely chopped hazelnuts

1. Preheat the oven to 350°F. Lightly butter and flour a large baking sheet.

2. In a medium-size bowl, beat the 2 eggs with a fork until they are foamy. Add the vanilla brandy. Slowly add the vanilla sugar and salt, mixing with a fork until blended.

3. Sift the flour and baking powder into a large bowl. Make a well in the center of the dry ingredients. Pour the egg mixture into the well and mix with a fork until the flour is moistened and the mixture is crumbly.

4. Turn the dough out onto a lightly floured surface. Knead it gently, gradually adding the hazelnuts. When the dough is smooth, divide it in half.

5. Shape each dough half into a log 16 inches long and about 1 inch in diameter. Arrange the logs on the prepared baking sheet about 2 inches apart. Lightly beat the egg white and brush the logs with it.

6. Bake the dough in the preheated oven for 25 to 30 minutes, until the logs are golden brown. Cool them

on the baking sheet on a wire rack for 15 minutes. Reduce the oven temperature to 300°F.

7. Remove the logs from the baking sheet and cut them in diagonal slices ½ inch thick. Stand the slices upright on the same baking sheet.

8. Bake the biscotti at 300°F for 20 minutes, until they are dry and lightly golden. Cool them on the sheet set on a rack. (They will be crisp throughout.)

9. Store the biscotti in an airtight container for up to several weeks.

BENNE SEED BISCUITS

MAKES 5 DOZEN

Benne seeds were brought to this country by African slaves, and the seeds were used widely in Southern cooking as a result. Now more commonly known as sesame seeds, they are found in both sweet and savory dishes.

1 cup benne seeds	1 teaspoon salt, plus additional for sprinkling
3 cups all-purpose flour	⅔ cup cold lard or shortening, cut in small pieces
1½ teaspoons single-acting baking powder (see Note for Buttermilk Biscuits, page 117)	⅔ cup milk

1. Preheat the oven to 425°F.

2. Spread the benne seeds in a shallow pan and bake for 5 minutes, or until the seeds turn the color of butterscotch. Watch the seeds carefully to keep them from burning and stir them occasionally.

3. Sift the flour, baking powder, and 1 teaspoon of the salt into a large bowl. With a pastry blender or two knives, cut in the lard until the mixture resembles cornmeal.

4. Make a well in the center of the mixture. Pour in the milk all at once. Mix thoroughly. Stir in the benne seeds.

5. On a floured surface, knead the dough for a few seconds, then shape it into 2 balls.

6. Dust a rolling pin with flour. On a floured surface, roll out half the dough at a time, to a thickness of $\frac{1}{16}$ inch. Using a 2-inch biscuit cutter dipped in flour, cut out biscuits.

7. Arrange the biscuits ¼ inch apart on an unbuttered baking sheet or a baking sheet that has been lined with parchment paper.

8. Bake for 12 minutes, until lightly browned. Remove the biscuits from the pan. Sprinkle with a little salt and serve hot.

TEAPOT MOTIFS

Thomas Twining, one of the world's most famous names in tea, originally opened a coffeehouse in London in 1706. At the time, the city had more than two thousand such establishments. To compete, Twining decided to serve tea. The original shop on The Strand now houses a tea museum featuring ornate tea caddies, an unusual double-spouted teapot, scales, and decorated tins.

BUTTERMILK BISCUITS

MAKES 3 1/2 DOZEN

For this recipe, chef and Virginia native Edna Lewis makes her own single-acting baking powder, which releases its leavening power when it is moistened. (Double-acting baking powder releases some of its leavening power when it gets wet and the rest when it gets hot.) Biscuits like these, flaky and light, are the pride of many a Southern baker.

3⅔ cups unbleached all-purpose flour

2 tablespoons single-acting baking powder

2 teaspoons salt

4 ounces cold lard or shortening, cut in small pieces

1 cup plus 2 tablespoons buttermilk or sour milk

1. Preheat the oven to 450°F.

2. In a large bowl, combine the flour, baking powder, and salt. Mix well. With a pastry blender or two knives, quickly cut in the lard until the mixture resembles cornmeal.

3. Make a well in center of the mixture. Pour in the milk all at once. Stir vigorously for a few seconds with a wooden spoon just until moistened.

4. Work the dough into a ball. Turn it out onto a floured surface and knead vigorously for just 3 seconds. Shape the dough into a disk.

5. Dust a rolling pin with flour. Roll the dough out on a floured surface to a thickness of ¼ inch. Pierce the surface of the dough all over with a fork. Starting with the outer edge of the dough, cut out biscuits using a 2-inch biscuit cutter dipped in flour. For straight-sided biscuits, do not wiggle the cutter. Press straight down and pull up sharply.

6. Place the biscuits ¼ inch apart on a heavy unbuttered baking sheet with a shiny surface or on two thin baking sheets stacked and covered with a piece of foil shiny side up.

7. Bake for 12 to 13 minutes, just until light golden blond. Remove the biscuits from the oven and let them stand a few minutes. Serve hot. The biscuits can be reheated, uncovered, at 375°F for 4 to 5 minutes.

NOTE: To make single-acting baking powder, combine 2 ounces cream of tartar, 1 ounce baking soda, and ½ ounce cornstarch in a small bowl. Mix well. Store the powder in an airtight container. To substitute sour milk for the buttermilk, pour 1 tablespoon cider vinegar into a 2-cup measuring cup. Add milk to the 1-cup line, then add 2 additional tablespoons milk. Mix well.

Feather-Light Biscuits with Country Ham

MAKES 1 1/2 DOZEN

A Southern treat, to be sure, is a little sandwich of country ham on a biscuit. This version is served by Curtis Grace, chef and proprietor at Ninth Street House, a restaurant in a charming old turreted house in Paducah, Kentucky.

BISCUITS

2 cups all-purpose flour

I tablespoon baking powder

I tablespoon sugar

I teaspoon salt

¼ cup shortening

I envelope active dry yeast

¾ cup warm (110°F) milk

Unsalted butter, melted

COUNTRY HAM FILLING

I cup ground cooked
   country ham

3 tablespoons mayonnaise

½ teaspoon dry mustard

½ teaspoon prepared
   horseradish

Unsalted butter, softened

1. To make the biscuits, sift the flour, baking powder, sugar, and salt into a large bowl. With two knives, cut in the shortening until the mixture resembles coarse meal. Make a well in the center.

2. In a small bowl, sprinkle the yeast over ¼ cup warm (110°F) water. Stir until the yeast dissolves. Add the milk and mix well. Pour into the well of the dry ingredients. Stir with a fork until moistened. The dough will be sticky.

3. Turn the dough onto a heavily floured surface. Knead gently with floured fingertips for 30 seconds, until the dough is smooth.

4. Cover the dough with a tea towel and let it rise about 20 minutes.

5. Gently roll out the dough ½ inch thick. Cut biscuits with a floured 2½-inch heart-shaped cutter. Arrange the biscuits 2 inches apart on an unbuttered baking sheet.

6. Preheat the oven to 400°F. Let the biscuits rise at room temperature for 15 minutes.

7. Bake the biscuits until brown, 12 to 15 minutes.

8. Brush the tops of the hot biscuits with melted butter. Cool on a rack.

9. To make the filling, mix together the ground ham, mayonnaise, mustard, and horseradish in a bowl.

10. To serve, split the biscuits open and lightly butter the halves. Use 2 tablespoons of filling for each sandwich.

NOTE: To make ahead, prepare and cut the dough as above. Cover and refrigerate the unbaked biscuits on an unbuttered baking sheet for up to 24 hours. To bake: Let the biscuits rise in a warm place for 30 minutes. Bake and fill as above. The filling may be refrigerated for 24 hours.

CHÈVRE HERB CRISPS

MAKES 4 DOZEN

1 (17¼-ounce) package frozen puff pastry, thawed (2 sheets)

12 ounces chèvre, at room temperature

6 tablespoons unsalted butter, softened

2 tablespoons chopped chives

2 tablespoons chopped parsley

1 teaspoon coarsely ground pepper

Salt to taste

1. Preheat the oven to 350°F.

2. Gently unfold 1 sheet of pastry on a lightly floured surface. Press the pastry together at the two seams to seal. Roll the pastry out to a 14 by 11-inch rectangle. Trim the pastry to make the edges even. Repeat with the remaining pastry sheet.

3. Line two baking sheets with parchment paper. Arrange each pastry rectangle on a prepared sheet and prick them all over with a fork. To keep the pastry flat during baking, cover each rectangle with another sheet of parchment paper and another baking sheet.

4. Bake the pastry in the preheated oven for 30 minutes. Remove the top baking sheet and parchment paper from each pastry. Bake the pastry 3 to 5 minutes longer, until it is evenly browned. Cool the pastry on the baking sheets on wire racks.

5. While the pastry is cooling, combine the chèvre and butter in the small bowl of an electric mixer. Beat at medium speed until the mixture is light and fluffy. Stir in the chives, parsley, and pepper and season with salt.

6. Place 1 sheet of cooled pastry on a large board. Spread with the chèvre filling. Top with the remaining sheet of pastry. Press gently to seal and refrigerate for 1 hour, or until the filling is firm.

7. To serve, cut the pastry rectangle lengthwise into 6 equal strips about 1½ inches wide. Cut each strip diagonally into 1½-inch diamonds.

Marmalade Pumpkin Bread

MAKES 3 SMALL LOAVES

1½ cups all-purpose flour

½ cup granulated sugar

½ cup packed light brown sugar

1 tablespoon pumpkin pie spice

1½ teaspoons baking powder

½ teaspoon ground cinnamon

¼ teaspoon salt

3 eggs

⅔ cup canned pumpkin puree

⅓ cup unsalted butter, melted

¼ cup plus 2 tablespoons orange marmalade

3 tablespoons orange liqueur or orange juice

1. Butter and flour three loaf pans measuring 6 by 3 by 2 inches each. Preheat the oven to 350°F.
2. In a bowl, combine the flour, granulated sugar, brown sugar, pumpkin pie spice, baking powder, cinnamon, and salt. Mix well.
3. In the large bowl of an electric mixer, beat the eggs at medium speed until foamy. Beat in the pumpkin puree, the butter, ¼ cup of the marmalade, and 2 tablespoons of the liqueur until blended.
4. Gradually beat in the dry ingredients at low speed just until mixed. Spread the batter evenly in the loaf pans. Tap the pans sharply on a counter to release any air bubbles.
5. Bake the loaves on a baking sheet for 35 to 40 minutes, until a cake tester inserted in the center comes out clean. Cool the loaves in the pans on a rack for 10 minutes. Remove the bread from each pan and cool on a rack.
6. To make a glaze, mix the remaining 2 tablespoons of orange marmalade and 1 tablespoon of orange liqueur. Drizzle the glaze over the pumpkin bread. Wrap the cooled bread in foil or plastic wrap and store overnight before slicing.

Cherry Nut Bread

MAKES 1 LOAF

3 ounces dried pitted tart red cherries (about ½ cup)

1 tablespoon cherry brandy

2 cups all-purpose flour

1 cup sugar

1 tablespoon baking powder

Pinch of salt

¼ cup shortening

½ cup milk

1 tablespoon grated orange zest

¼ cup orange juice

2 eggs

½ cup chopped walnuts

1. Butter and flour an 8½ by 4½ by 2½-inch loaf pan. Line the bottom with waxed paper, then lightly butter and flour the paper. Preheat the oven to 350°F.

2. In a small bowl, toss the dried cherries with the brandy.

3. Sift the flour, sugar, baking powder, and salt into a large bowl. With a pastry blender or two knives, cut in the shortening until the mixture resembles coarse meal.

4. Make a well in the center of the flour mixture. Add the milk, orange zest and juice, and eggs. Stir with a fork until blended. Fold in the cherries and nuts. Pour the batter into the prepared pan.

5. Bake the bread for 60 to 65 minutes, until a cake tester inserted in the center comes out clean.

6. Cool in the pan set on a rack for 10 minutes. Run a knife around the edge to loosen the bread. Remove the bread from the pan, peel off the waxed paper, and cool on the rack.

ANGLERS & WRITERS MIXED FRUIT SCONES

MAKES 1 DOZEN

Although these days scones are often bursting with fruit, they are actually related to their plainer American cousin, the biscuit. In England, the classic teatime treat is scones topped with strawberry jam and rich clotted cream.

2 cups all-purpose flour

¼ cup plus 2 tablespoons sugar

4 teaspoons baking powder

Pinch of salt

¼ cup chopped dried apples

¼ cup chopped dried apricots

¼ cup chopped dried pitted tart red cherries or cranberries

¼ cup golden raisins

¼ cup finely chopped walnuts

1½ to 1¾ cups heavy cream

3 tablespoons unsalted butter, melted

Clotted cream, Lemon Curd (page 193), and Cherry Marmalade (page 193), for garnish

1. Butter two 9-inch pie plates. Preheat the oven to 350°F.

2. In a large bowl, combine the flour, ¼ cup of the sugar, the baking powder, and the salt. Mix well. Add the fruits and nuts. Toss until coated.

3. Gradually add the cream, stirring with a fork until a soft dough forms and the dough no longer sticks to the side of the bowl. Turn out onto a floured surface. Knead the dough 10 times with your fingertips.

121

4. Divide the dough in half. With a rolling pin dusted with flour, roll each half to a 7-inch circle, about ½ inch thick. Place the dough in the prepared pie plates.

5. Brush the top of the dough generously with the butter and sprinkle with the remaining 2 tablespoons of sugar. Using a sharp knife, score each circle of dough into 6 wedges.

6. Bake until browned, 25 to 30 minutes. Cut the scones into wedges along the scored lines. Serve hot with bowls of clotted cream, lemon curd, and cherry marmalade.

GINGER SCONES

MAKES 8 SCONES

Tête-à-têtes over tea and scones are a tradition in Terese Blanding's tea room in a 1912 house in McMinnville, Oregon, that's also her family's home. These scones, flavored with bits of crystallized ginger, have become a favorite.

2 cups all-purpose flour

1 tablespoon baking powder

2 tablespoons sugar, plus additional for garnish

¾ teaspoon salt

4 tablespoons unsalted butter

2 eggs, slightly beaten

⅓ cup heavy cream

½ cup crystallized ginger, chopped

1 egg white, slightly beaten

1. Preheat the oven to 400°F.

2. In a medium-size bowl, combine the flour, baking powder, sugar, and salt. Mix well. With a pastry blender, cut in the butter until the mixture resembles small peas.

3. Add the whole eggs and the cream. Stir until the dough clings together. Gather the dough into a ball. On a floured board, divide it in half. Add half the ginger to each piece of dough and knead it into the dough, adding a bit more flour if the dough is sticky.

4. Shape each dough half into a ball. Flatten each ball into a disk 4 inches in diameter and 1 inch thick. Cut each disk into 4 wedges.

5. Arrange the wedges 2 inches apart on an unbuttered baking sheet. Brush the tops of the scones with egg white and dust with sugar.

6. Bake for 20 to 25 minutes, until golden brown. Serve hot.

CUCUMBER SANDWICHES ON POTATO CHIVE BREAD

MAKES 1 DOZEN

4 tablespoons unsalted butter, softened

1 teaspoon chopped chives

1 teaspoon chopped dill

12 slices Potato Chive Bread (below) or firm-textured white bread

1 unwaxed cucumber, thinly sliced, lightly salted, and drained

Finely chopped chives, for garnish

1. In a small bowl, mix the butter with 2 teaspoons of the herbs.

2. Using a 2-inch biscuit cutter, cut 2 rounds from each slice of bread. Butter the rounds on one side with herb butter.

3. Top half the rounds with several cucumber slices and garnish generously with chopped chives. Cover each with a buttered round. Cover with damp paper towels and plastic wrap until ready to serve.

POTATO CHIVE BREAD

MAKES 1 LOAF

1 package active dry yeast

¾ cup warm (110°F) milk

4 cups all-purpose flour

1 teaspoon salt

2 medium-size potatoes, peeled, boiled, and mashed (2 cups)

3 tablespoons chopped chives

1. In a small bowl, sprinkle the yeast over ¼ cup of the warm milk. Let proof for 15 minutes, then stir until the yeast dissolves.

2. In a large bowl, combine the flour and salt. Cut in the mashed potatoes with a pastry blender.

3. Stir in the yeast mixture. Gradually stir in the remaining milk and ½ cup warm (110°F) water.

4. Turn the dough out onto a floured surface and knead it until it is smooth and elastic, about 8 minutes. Knead in the chives.

5. Butter a large bowl and turn the

dough over in it. Cover the bowl with a tea towel and let rise in a warm place for 1½ hours, until the dough has doubled in bulk.

6. Butter a 9 by 5 by 3-inch loaf pan. Punch the dough down and shape it into a loaf. Place it in the prepared loaf pan.

7. Cover the dough with a damp cloth and let it rise for 30 minutes. Preheat the oven to 375°F.

8. Bake the bread for 40 to 50 minutes, until the loaf sounds hollow when thumped on top. Remove the pan and cool the bread on a rack.

CHUTNEY CHEDDAR SANDWICHES ON WALNUT BREAD

MAKES 1 1/2 DOZEN

½ (8-ounce) package cream
    cheese, softened

I cup shredded cheddar cheese

2 tablespoons chutney

I teaspoon Dijon mustard

I scallion, thinly sliced

12 slices Walnut Bread (below)
    or whole-wheat bread, crusts
    removed

Unsalted butter, softened

Chopped parsley

1. In the small bowl of an electric mixer, beat the cream cheese, shredded cheddar cheese, chutney, mustard, and scallion at medium speed until blended.

2. Spread 6 bread slices with the cheese mixture. Top with the remaining bread slices. Cut each sandwich into 3 fingers.

3. Spread one end of each sandwich with butter and press it into the chopped parsley. Cover with damp paper towels and plastic wrap until ready to serve.

WALNUT BREAD

MAKES 1 LOAF

2 tablespoons honey

I package active dry yeast

I½ tablespoons walnut oil

I teaspoon salt

I½ cups whole-wheat flour

I cup ground walnuts

I½ cups all-purpose flour

I egg

1. In a large bowl, stir the honey into I cup warm (110°F) water until dissolved. Sprinkle the yeast over the water mixture and let it proof until dissolved, about 15 minutes.

2. Add the walnut oil and salt. Gradually stir in the whole-wheat flour, ground walnuts, and enough white flour to make a soft dough.

3. Turn the dough out on a floured surface and knead until smooth and elastic, about 8 minutes.

4. Butter a large bowl and turn the dough over in it. Cover dough with a towel and let it rise in a warm place until doubled in bulk, I¼ to I½ hours.

5. Punch down the dough and shape it into a loaf. Butter a 9 by 5 by 3-inch loaf pan. Put the dough in the pan and cover it with a tea towel. Let it rise until doubled in bulk, 30 to 45 minutes.

6. Preheat the oven to 350°F. In a bowl, whisk the egg with I tablespoon water. Brush over the loaf.

7. Bake the bread for 35 to 45 minutes, until the loaf sounds hollow when thumped. Remove from the pan and cool on a rack.

Tarragon Chicken Salad with Borage Blossoms

MAKES 1/2 DOZEN

1 cup finely chopped cooked chicken

2 tablespoons finely chopped, seeded, peeled cucumber

2 tablespoons finely chopped green bell pepper

1 tablespoon chopped fresh tarragon, or 1 teaspoon dried

1 tablespoon white wine vinegar

1 tablespoon vegetable oil

1 tablespoon mayonnaise

12 thin slices white or whole-wheat bread

Unsalted butter, softened

Borage blossoms, for garnish

1. In a medium-size bowl, combine the chicken, cucumber, green bell pepper, and tarragon.
2. In a small bowl, whisk together the vinegar, oil, and mayonnaise until blended. Stir the dressing into the chicken mixture.
3. Spread the bread lightly with butter. Using a 3-inch heart-shaped cookie cutter, cut a heart from each slice of bread.
4. Make 6 sandwiches. Decorate the center of each sandwich with borage blossoms, if desired.

Tuna Sandwiches with Thyme Blossoms

MAKES 1/2 DOZEN

1 (6-ounce) can water-packed tuna, drained and flaked

3 tablespoons mayonnaise

1½ teaspoons lemon juice

¼ cup finely chopped celery

2 to 3 tablespoons chopped chives

2 tablespoons fresh thyme, or 1 teaspoon dried

Salt and pepper to taste

12 thin slices whole-wheat bread

Thyme blossoms, for garnish

1. In a small bowl, mix the tuna, mayonnaise, and lemon juice. Stir in the celery, chives, and thyme. Season with salt and pepper.
2. With a cookie cutter, cut a 3-inch circle from each slice of bread. Using a ½-inch miniature cutter or a thimble, cut an opening in the center of half the bread rounds.
3. Spread tuna salad on each solid round of bread. Top with a cutout bread round. Tuck a few thyme flowers into each opening for garnish and serve.

TEA SANDWICHES

The Fourth Earl of Sandwich was looking for food easy enough to eat at the gaming table, and the sandwich was born. Adapted for the gentle ritual of tea, these little sandwiches are models of invention: chicken salad with rosemary, tuna with a touch of thyme, shrimp with pesto and tiny strips of orange zest. Treat each sandwich as a work of art, using cookie cutters, edible blossoms, or strips of sun-dried tomatoes for decoration. Or moisten the edge of a sandwich with mayonnaise and dip it in finely minced parsley. Arrange the sandwiches on tiered servers or cake stands.

BORAGE & BURNET

The flavor of both borage and salad burnet is reminiscent of cucumber. The bright flowers and the leaves of borage are used in iced drinks and salads, but the leaves must be finely chopped. In times past, borage was thought to endow those who ate it with courage. Salad burnet ~ actually an herb, also known as garden burnet ~ was popular in Elizabethan times. Its leaves, used in sauces, salads, and teas, are best when they are young, but they can be finely chopped and frozen. You can grow them yourself, or try farmers' markets and specialty gardeners.

Egg Salad with Salad Burnet & Chive Blossoms

MAKES 1 DOZEN

12 thin slices white bread
Unsalted butter, softened
6 hard-cooked eggs
2 or 3 tablespoons mayonnaise to taste
1 tablespoon sour cream
¼ cup chopped, seeded, peeled cucumber

2 tablespoons chopped salad burnet (if unavailable, use an additional 1 tablespoon chopped chives)
2 tablespoons chopped chives
Salt and pepper to taste
Chive blossoms, for garnish

1. Spread the bread lightly with the butter. Using a flower-shaped cookie cutter, cut 12 flowers from the bread slices.
2. In a bowl, chop the hard-cooked eggs. Stir in the mayonnaise and sour cream. Fold in the cucumber, salad burnet, and chives. Season with salt and pepper.
3. Spread the egg salad on the bread cutouts. Arrange chive blossoms in a circle in the center of each sandwich to resemble a flower.

Grilled Chicken with Watercress Sandwiches

MAKES 4 DOZEN

1 pound boned, skinned chicken breasts
½ cup mayonnaise
1 tablespoon chopped fresh basil, or 1 teaspoon dried
1 tablespoon chopped fresh rosemary, or 1 teaspoon dried

¼ teaspoon finely minced garlic
12 thin slices white bread, crusts removed
1 bunch watercress
Salt and pepper to taste

1. Grill the chicken over hot coals and chips of dried mesquite, or broil it in a broiler until the juices run clear. Cool the chicken and cut it into thin slices.
2. In a small bowl, mix together the mayonnaise, basil, rosemary, and garlic.
3. Spread the mayonnaise mixture on the bread slices. Layer sliced chicken and sprigs of watercress on the bread. Season with salt and white pepper. Cut each sandwich twice diagonally to make four triangles.

Chèvre, Sun-Dried Tomato & Basil Sandwiches

MAKES 1 DOZEN

1 (6-ounce) log chèvre

2 to 4 tablespoons heavy cream

½ cup chopped basil

½ garlic clove (optional)

Salt and pepper to taste

12 thin slices white bread

12 oil-packed, sun-dried tomatoes, drained and cut in 5 strips each

Edible herb blossoms, for garnish

1. In the small bowl of an electric mixer, mash the chèvre. Add the cream and beat at medium speed until light and smooth.

2. Stir in the basil. If using, add the garlic through a press. Season the mixture with salt and pepper.

3. Cut a star shape from each slice of bread, then spread the slices with the chèvre mixture.

4. Arrange 5 strips of sun-dried tomato on each sandwich so the slices radiate from the center toward the points. Garnish each with an herb blossom.

Tomato Provençal Sandwiches

MAKES 1 DOZEN

24 thin slices white bread

Mayonnaise

3 small ripe tomatoes, cut in 4 slices each

1 tablespoon chopped basil

1 tablespoon chopped marjoram

1 tablespoon chopped oregano

1 tablespoon chopped thyme

Salt and pepper to taste

Edible herb blossoms, for garnish

1. Cut a circle the same size as the tomato slices from each bread slice.

2. Spread the bread rounds with mayonnaise, then top 12 of them with a tomato slice.

3. Mix together the basil, marjo-ram, oregano, and thyme. Sprinkle the herbs over the tomato slices. Season with salt and pepper. Top each sandwich with the remaining bread rounds.

4. Decorate with herb blossoms.

Menus to Remember

TEA FOR GOOD FRIENDS

Violet Kir

PAGE 182

Afternoon Tea

PAGE 140

Assorted Tea Sandwiches

PAGES 124-130

Anglers & Writers Mixed Fruit Scones

PAGE 121

Ginger Cream Cookie Sandwiches

PAGE 132

Lemon Bars

PAGE 132

Fruit Barquettes

PAGE 74

Sage & Cheddar Cheese Melties

MAKES 4 DOZEN
OPEN-FACE SANDWICHES

I cup shredded cheddar cheese

½ teaspoon dried sage

12 thin slices white bread, crusts removed

Mayonnaise

Sage blossoms or leaves, for garnish

1. In a medium-size bowl, combine the cheese and sage. Spread the bread lightly with mayonnaise, then sprinkle with the cheese mixture.

2. Cut each slice into 4 triangles. Arrange on two baking sheets.

3. Preheat an electric broiler. (It is not necessary to preheat a gas broiler.) In two batches, broil the sandwiches 3 inches from the heat until the cheese is melted and beginning to brown, about I minute. (Or grill the sandwiches in a toaster oven.)

4. Decorate each sandwich with a sage blossom or sage leaves.

Lemon Cream Nasturtium Sandwiches

MAKES 1 DOZEN

12 thin slices white or whole-wheat bread

I (3-ounce) package cream cheese, softened

2 tablespoons milk

I tablespoon lemon juice

Grated zest of I lemon

12 large pesticide-free nasturtium leaves and flowers

1. Cut a circle the same size as a nasturtium leaf from each bread slice.

2. In the small bowl of an electric mixer, beat the cream cheese, milk, and lemon juice at medium speed until smooth and fluffy. Stir in the lemon zest.

3. Spread the bread rounds lightly with some of the cheese mixture. Cover with a nasturtium leaf.

4. Dab a bit of cheese mixture on the underside of each flower, then secure the blossoms on the leaves.

Lemon Bars

MAKES 2 DOZEN

3 cups unbleached all-purpose flour

⅔ cup confectioners' sugar, plus additional for sprinkling

1 cup (2 sticks) cold unsalted butter, cut in small pieces

4 tablespoons cold margarine, cut in small pieces

5 eggs

2½ cups granulated sugar

6 tablespoons lemon juice

¾ teaspoon baking soda

1. Preheat the oven to 350°F. In the large bowl of an electric mixer, combine 2½ cups of the flour, the ⅔ cup confectioners' sugar, the butter, and the margarine. Beat at low speed for about 1 minute, then at medium speed until the mixture turns to crumbs. Press the crumbs into an unbuttered 15 by 10 by 1-inch jelly-roll pan.

2. Bake for 15 to 20 minutes, until the crust is firm but not brown.

3. Using clean beaters, beat the eggs, granulated sugar, and lemon juice in the small bowl of an elec-tric mixer until smooth. Mix the remaining ½ cup flour and baking soda together and add that to the egg mixture. Beat just until blend-ed. Pour the filling over the hot crust. The pan will be very full.

4. Bake for 25 minutes, until the filling is set and lightly browned. The edges will begin to pull away from the sides of the pan. Cool the pan on a wire rack.

5. Sprinkle the surface with con-fectioners' sugar. Cut into 6 squares, then cut each square in quarters to make four triangles.

Ginger Cream Cookie Sandwiches

MAKES 1 1/2 DOZEN

A tireless lover of ginger, Pittsburgh journalist Marlene Parrish serves her cookies with gingerade, made by melt-ing ginger crystals and mixing the syrup with sparkling water.

2 cups all-purpose flour

1½ teaspoons baking powder

1 teaspoon ground ginger

1 teaspoon ground cinnamon

¼ teaspoon baking soda

¼ teaspoon ground cloves

¼ cup buttermilk

1 teaspoon cider vinegar

¾ cup (1½ sticks) unsalted butter, softened

½ cup packed light brown sugar

½ cup molasses

1 egg

¼ cup minced crystallized ginger

1 cup sifted confectioners' sugar, plus additional for garnish

1. Preheat the oven to 350°F. Butter two baking sheets.

2. Sift together the flour, baking powder, ground ginger, cinnamon, baking soda, and cloves.

3. In a 1-cup measuring cup, combine the buttermilk and the cider vinegar. Mix well.

4. In the small bowl of an electric mixer, beat ½ cup of the butter and the brown sugar at medium speed until light and fluffy.

5. Beat in the molasses, egg, and 3 tablespoons of the flour mixture until smooth. Beat in the remaining dry ingredients alternately with the buttermilk mixture, beating at low speed until blended after each addition.

6. Drop the batter by rounded teaspoonfuls 2 inches apart on the prepared baking sheets.

7. Bake for 14 to 16 minutes, until the tops spring back when lightly touched. Remove the cookies from the baking sheets to racks to cool.

8. In the small bowl of an electric mixer, beat the remaining ¼ cup of butter, the crystallized ginger, and 1 cup of confectioners' sugar until well blended.

9. Spread the bottoms of half the cookies with the ginger frosting, using about ½ tablespoon for each. Press the bottoms of the remaining cookies onto the frosting to make sandwiches. To garnish, sift confectioners' sugar over the cookie tops.

TEXAS GOLD BARS

MAKES 2 TO 3 DOZEN

⅔ cup confectioners' sugar

2 cups all-purpose flour

1 cup (2 sticks) unsalted butter, softened, plus ⅔ cup melted

½ cup honey

3 tablespoons heavy cream

1 teaspoon vanilla extract

½ cup packed light brown sugar

3½ cups coarsely chopped pecans

1. Butter a 13 by 9 by 2-inch baking pan. Preheat the oven to 350°F.

2. Sift the confectioners' sugar and flour into a large bowl. With a pastry blender or two knives, cut in the softened butter until the mixture is fine and crumbly. Pat it firmly into the bottom of the prepared pan to form a crust.

3. Bake for 20 minutes. Meanwhile, in a medium-size bowl, combine the melted butter, honey, cream, vanilla, and brown sugar. Mix until blended. Stir in the pecans. Spread the topping over the hot crust.

4. Bake for 25 minutes, or until the center is bubbling.

5. Cool on a rack, then refrigerate for several hours until the pecan mixture is firm. Cut into bars. Store tightly wrapped in the refrigerator. Let the bars stand at room temperature for 1 hour before serving.

Almond Tuiles

MAKES 1 1/2 DOZEN

Tuile (the word in French means "tile") is a cookie that is molded while still hot from the oven over a tube or rolling pin to resemble a roof tile. It can also serve as an ice cream or sorbet cup if it is shaped, while hot, in a muffin cup.

½ cup (I stick) unsalted
  butter, softened
I cup sugar
4 egg whites
I teaspoon almond extract
I cup all-purpose flour
I cup sliced almonds

1. Preheat the oven to 375°F. Line two baking sheets with parchment paper. Make a template for shaping the tuiles: Draw a circle 6 inches in diameter on a 7-inch square of cardboard. Cut out the circle, leaving a round hole in a square card.
2. In the small bowl of an electric mixer, beat the butter, sugar, egg whites, almond extract, and flour at medium speed until blended.
3. Make the tuiles in batches. Set the template in a corner of the baking sheet. Spoon 2 tablespoons of the batter into the center of the circle. Spread the batter out with a spatula to fill the circle. Sprinkle each circle of batter with about I tablespoon of sliced almonds.

4. Bake the tuiles for 6 to 8 minutes, until the edges turn golden.
5. Open the oven door and set the baking sheet on it so that the tuiles are kept hot but do not bake any more; they are easy to mold when hot, but become hard as soon as they cool. Loosen the tuiles from the parchment paper with a metal spatula, then shape them in one of the following ways: To make wafers, lay the tuiles on a rolling pin. To make tubes, wrap the tuiles around the handle of a spoon. To make cups (called tulipes), gently press them into muffin cups. Or form cornucopias by rolling hot tuiles into a cone shape.

Miniature Swiss Jelly Rolls

MAKES 1 1/2 DOZEN SLICES

I cup unbleached all-purpose
  flour
½ teaspoon baking powder
4 eggs
½ cup superfine sugar
Confectioners' sugar
⅔ cup blackberry jam
Blackberries and pesticide-free
  rose petals, for garnish

TEA TRADITIONS

It may never be too soon to teach children the traditions of afternoon tea. Expect eager students, for youngsters have long loved playing at tea parties, and will no doubt love the real thing even more. If they dress up in their best clothes, children ~ even the boys ~ will be more likely to be on their best behavior. And what small hand can resist the special little sandwiches and cakes that adorn the tea table?

1. Preheat the oven to 425°F. Line the bottom of a 15 by 10 by 1-inch jelly-roll pan with parchment paper and butter the parchment.
2. Sift the flour and baking powder into a small bowl.
3. In the large bowl of an electric mixer, beat the eggs and superfine sugar at high speed until thick and creamy, about 5 minutes. Gradually sprinkle the flour mixture over the egg mixture, then fold in gently with a rubber spatula. Be sure there are no dry pockets of flour. Fold in 1 tablespoon of water.
4. Pour the batter into the pan. Spread evenly, smoothing the top.
5. Bake the cake for 10 minutes, or until the center springs back when lightly touched. While the cake is baking, sprinkle a 20-inch-long sheet of parchment paper with sifted confectioners' sugar.
6. Remove the cake from the oven and immediately run a knife around the edges to loosen, then invert the hot cake onto the sugared paper. Peel off the parchment from the bottom of the cake. Trim off crusty edges with a knife.
7. Cut both the cake and the parchment in half crosswise. Gently roll up each hot cake in parchment starting from the narrow end, then wrap in a clean, warm, damp cloth. Cool on a rack.
8. Before serving, gently unroll the cakes. Spread each cake with half the jam, leaving a 1-inch border on all sides. Reroll the cakes, cover, and refrigerate for at least 1 hour.
9. Cut each cake into 9 slices and garnish each slice with blackberries and rose petals.

BUTTERFLY FAIRY CAKES

MAKES 32 CAKES

These tiny cakes, with sugar-sprinkled butterfly wings, will seem as if delivered by a fairy. Surprisingly, it's a fairly simple trick that transforms them from ordinary cupcakes into a perfect treat for a children's tea party.

1½ cups unbleached all-purpose flour

2 teaspoons baking powder

1 cup (2 sticks) unsalted butter, softened

¾ cup superfine sugar

2 eggs, beaten

2 tablespoons milk

1½ cups confectioners' sugar

1 teaspoon vanilla extract

Colored sugar crystals, for garnish

1. Butter 32 mini-muffin cups (1¾ inches in diameter) or line them with paper liners. Preheat the oven to 375°F.
2. Sift together the flour and the baking powder.
3. In the small bowl of an electric mixer, cream ½ cup of the butter

at medium speed. Gradually add the superfine sugar, beating until light and fluffy. Add the beaten eggs, a little at a time, beating well after each addition.

4. Fold in the flour mixture. Stir in the milk until the dough becomes stiff dropping consistency. Spoon the dough into the muffin cups, filling each three quarters full.

5. Bake the cakes in the upper third of the oven for 15 minutes, or until a cake tester inserted in the center comes out clean. Cool in the pan set on a rack. Remove the cakes from the pan.

6. In the bowl of a food processor, process the remaining ½ cup of butter until creamy. With the processor running, gradually add the confectioners' sugar and vanilla, processing until blended.

7. Cut a ¼-inch-thick slice from the top of each cupcake. Spoon a dollop of filling on the bottom portion of each cake.

8. Cut each cake-top slice in half. Dip the cut sides of the cake tops in colored sugar crystals. Replace the top cake pieces, sugared side up, at an angle in the cream filling, forming the butterfly's wings.

VANILLA CREAM CAKE

SERVES 12 TO 16

2¼ cups cake flour
2¼ teaspoons baking powder
½ teaspoon salt
1 cup heavy cream
1 tablespoon Vanilla Brandy (page 187)

4 eggs
1¼ cups Vanilla Sugar (page 70)
Confectioners' sugar, for garnish

1. Butter and flour a 10-inch tube pan. Line the bottom of the pan with waxed paper, then butter and flour the paper. Preheat the oven to 350°F.

2. In a medium-size bowl, stir together the flour, baking powder, and salt. Mix well and set aside.

3. In the small bowl of an electric mixer, beat the heavy cream and vanilla brandy until stiff. Cover and refrigerate while mixing the batter.

4. With clean beaters, beat the eggs in the large bowl of the mixer at high speed until they are foamy. Gradually add the vanilla sugar, beating until the mixture is thick and

lemon colored, about 5 minutes.

5. Add the flour mixture all at once. Beat at low speed until the ingredients are moistened. Fold in the whipped cream. Pour the batter into the prepared pan and place the pan on a baking sheet.

6. Bake the cake on the bottom rack of the preheated oven for 55 to 60 minutes, until a cake tester inserted in the center of the cake comes out clean. (The cake will not fill the pan.) Cool the cake on a rack.

7. To serve, invert the cake on a platter and remove the pan. Peel off the waxed paper and dust the cake with confectioners' sugar.

Menus to Remember

CHILDREN'S TEA PARTY

Bacon Quiche Tartlets
PAGE 104

Marmalade Pumpkin Bread
PAGE 120

Butterfly Fairy Cakes
PAGE 135

Strawberry Cream Cheese
PAGE 148

Miniature Swiss Jelly Rolls
PAGE 134

A SOOTHING TONIC

*No matter how brief,
a pause for herbal tea
lends a note of luxury and
calm to the day. Share
a warming pot with friends
over cakes and sandwiches,
or enjoy a solitary
cup of chilled herbal tea on a
sultry summer afternoon.
Good flavors to try:
sage, mint, lavender, rosemary,
and lemon verbena.*

CAKE

2 cups cake flour

1 tablespoon baking powder

¼ teaspoon salt

4 tablespoons unsalted butter, softened

¼ cup vegetable shortening

1¼ cups granulated sugar

½ teaspoon vanilla extract

¼ teaspoon almond extract

¾ cup milk

6 egg whites

½ cup apricot jam

ICING

2 tablespoons light corn syrup

Few drops vanilla extract

6 cups confectioners' sugar, sifted

BUTTERCREAM

4 tablespoons unsalted butter, softened

2 cups confectioners' sugar, sifted

½ teaspoon almond extract

½ teaspoon vanilla extract

2 tablespoons light cream

Food coloring, for garnish

Silver and gold dragées, for garnish

1. To make the cake, butter and flour a 13 by 9 by 2-inch baking pan. Line the bottom with waxed paper, then butter and flour the waxed paper. Preheat the oven to 350°F.

2. Sift together the flour, baking powder, and salt.

3. In the large bowl of an electric mixer, cream 4 tablespoons butter, the shortening, and 1 cup of the granulated sugar at medium speed until light and fluffy, scraping the side of the bowl often. Add ½ teaspoon vanilla and ¼ teaspoon almond extract. Add the flour mixture alternately with the milk, beating until smooth after each addition.

4. In the small bowl of an electric mixer, using clean beaters, beat the egg whites until very frothy. Gradually beat in the remaining ¼ cup of granulated sugar, beating to soft peaks. Fold the whites into the batter. Spread the batter in the pan.

5. Bake the cake for 35 to 40 min-

utes, until a cake tester inserted in the center comes out clean. Cool on a rack for 10 minutes. Remove the cake from the pan, peel off the paper, and cool on a rack.

6. In a small saucepan, stir the jam over medium heat until melted.

7. Trim all the crust from the top, bottom, and sides of the cake. Brush off any loose crumbs. Cut the cake into 2-inch rounds or into rectangles with perfectly straight sides. Cut the cake pieces in half crosswise. Spread a thin layer of jam between the layers.

8. Arrange the cake pieces 3 to 4 inches apart on a rack set over a baking sheet.

9. To make the icing, combine ½ cup plus 1 tablespoon of water with the corn syrup and a few drops of vanilla in a heavy large saucepan. Gradually stir in the 6 cups confectioners' sugar. Mix well. Stir constantly over medium heat until the icing is warm (110°F).

10. Gently pour the icing over the cakes, tilting the baking sheet to coat the sides evenly. Allow to set a few minutes, then continue spooning the icing from the baking sheet over the cakes. Give the cakes three or four coats so the icing forms a smooth, mirror-like finish. (The icing will thicken while standing. Reheat it with a little water.)

11. Let the icing become firm. Place the cakes on a baking sheet lined with waxed paper.

12. To make the buttercream, beat 4 tablespoons butter in the small bowl of an electric mixer at medium speed. Gradually add the 2 cups confectioners' sugar, ½ teaspoon almond extract, and ½ teaspoon vanilla.

13. Beat in enough cream to make the buttercream spreadable.

14. Divide the buttercream into small bowls. Add a few drops of food coloring to each as desired.

15. Pipe flowers and leaves of buttercream on the cakes using pastry bags and decorating tubes. Center silver or gold dragées on the flowers.

16. After the buttercream has set, cover the cakes. They can be stored at room temperature for several days.

SHERRY

Sherry recalls things British, to be sure, things refined and sophisticated. Sherry was brought to England from Spain in the early sixteenth century. Literary characters have shown a fondness for it, including the "sack" of Shakespeare's Falstaff and Poe's "Cask of Amontillado."

MADELEINES

MAKES 2 DOZEN

3 eggs, plus 1 egg yolk
⅔ cup superfine sugar
2 tablespoons lemon juice
1 teaspoon vanilla extract
Pinch of salt

1¼ cups sifted all-purpose flour
½ cup (1 stick) unsalted butter, melted
24 lemon balm leaves

1. Preheat the oven to 375°F. Spray 24 madeleine molds with a non-stick coating.

2. In the small bowl of an electric mixer, beat the eggs and yolk and the sugar at high speed until pale and thick, about 5 minutes.

3. Beat in the lemon juice, vanilla, and salt. Gradually fold in the flour until it is well mixed. Drizzle the butter over the batter and thoroughly fold it in.

4. Cover the bowl, and refrigerate the batter for 30 minutes.

5. Spoon 1 tablespoon batter into each mold. Do not spread the batter out. Top each mound of batter with a lemon balm leaf. Spoon 1 tablespoon batter over each leaf to cover completely.

6. Bake the madeleines on a baking sheet for 20 to 25 minutes, until the edges are lightly browned and a cake tester inserted into the center of one madeleine comes out clean.

7. Carefully loosen the edges of the madeleines with a knife. Invert onto a rack to cool. Madeleines are best served the day they are baked.

139

TEA

"There is very little art in making good tea; if the water is boiling, and there is no sparing of the fragrant leaf, the beverage will invariably be good. The old-fashioned plan of allowing a teaspoonful to each person, and one over, is still practiced. Warm the teapot with boiling water . . . for two or three minutes . . . then pour it away. Put in the tea, pour in one-half to three-quarters pint of 'boiling' water, close the lid, and let it stand for the tea to draw from five to ten minutes; then fill up the pot with water. The tea will be quite spoiled unless made with water that is 'actually boiling,' as the leaves will not open and the flavor will not be extracted from them."

ISABELLA BEETON
Book of Household Management

AFTERNOON TEA

SERVES 8

¼ cup dried lemon verbena
2 tablespoons orange pekoe tea
2 tablespoons dried orange zest

Combine the lemon verbena, tea, and orange zest in a teapot. Pour 8 cups of boiling water over the tea mixture. Cover and allow to steep for 5 to 7 minutes. Strain the tea and serve hot.

ORANGE CLOVE TEA

SERVES 4

3 to 4 teaspoons
orange-pekoe tea

I orange, rinsed, dried, and
cut in ½-inch-thick slices
Whole cloves

I. Warm a teapot and teacups with hot water. Drain and dry them.
2. Put the tea leaves in the teapot. Add I quart of boiling water. Cover and steep for 5 minutes.
3. Cut each orange slice in half so that each piece is a semicircle. Stud the skin side with several whole cloves. Put an orange slice in the bottom of each teacup.
4. Stir and strain the tea into warmed cups. Serve immediately.

ICED LEMON BALM TEA

SERVES 6

I bunch (I ½ to 2 ounces) fresh
lemon balm
I small lemon, thinly sliced

4 mint tea bags
3 tablespoons honey

I. Reserve 6 sprigs of lemon balm for garnish. Combine the remaining lemon balm, lemon slices, and mint tea in a teapot. Pour in 2 cups of boiling water. Cover and steep for 5 minutes.
2. Remove the tea bags. Stir in the honey. Cool to room temperature.
3. Strain the tea into a large pitcher or decanter. Add 4 cups of cold water and stir well. Refrigerate until serving, then pour the cold tea over ice in tall glasses. Garnish with the reserved lemon balm.

Rose Almond Milk

SERVES 4

One sip of this combination of milk, almond extract, and rose water and you could believe you live in an earlier time and place. Old-fashioned this may be, but its refreshing qualities have a modern power to soothe. If children are included in your party, they'll love this cooler.

2 teaspoons rose water, or 6 pesticide-free rose geranium leaves

I quart milk

I teaspoon almond extract

Pesticide-free rose geranium leaves or blossoms, for garnish

1. If you are using rose geranium leaves, cut them in pieces and place them in a small saucepan with 2 cups of milk. Scald the milk. Remove the leaves from the heat and let them steep, covered, until cool. Strain the cooled milk into a pitcher.
2. Stir in the remaining milk and the almond extract.

3. If you are using rose water, mix it in a pitcher with the milk and almond extract.
4. Serve the milk over ice, or whir 2 cups of the milk mixture in a blender with ½ cup of cracked ice before serving. Garnish with rose geranium leaves.

Classic Lemonade

SERVES 4

I½ cups sugar

I tablespoon finely grated lemon zest

I½ cups lemon juice (6 to 8 lemons)

Cold water or sparkling water

Lemon slices and mint sprigs, for garnish

1. In a medium-size saucepan, heat I½ cups water until almost boiling. Remove from the heat. Add the sugar and lemon zest and stir until the sugar is dissolved. Add the lemon juice and stir to mix well.

Cover and refrigerate until cold.
2. Combine equal parts of the lemon syrup and cold water. Serve the lemonade in a tall glass over ice. Garnish with lemon slices and mint sprigs, if desired.

MINT

Soothe your weariness with a cup of mint tea, or dress up breakfast juice with a sprig of mint. A hearty and abundant herb, mint has myriad uses ~ in candies, spearmint jelly, mint juleps ~ and appears in many savory dishes of the Middle East. Steeped in water, it can make a refreshing room or body spray, and mint infusions are said to ease indigestion and other maladies.

TEA FRUIT PUNCH

MAKES 25 CUPS

4 cups sugar
8 cups weak tea
6 cups peach nectar
4 cups orange juice
I cup lemon juice

I (750 ml) bottle cold
   ginger ale
Peach slices and pesticide-free
   nasturtium blossoms and
   leaves, for garnish

1. In a medium-size saucepan, combine the sugar with 1½ cups of cold water. Bring the mixture to a boil, stirring to dissolve the sugar. Remove the sugar syrup from the heat and let it cool.

2. In a 2-gallon punch bowl, combine the sugar syrup, tea, peach nectar, orange juice, and lemon juice. Mix well. Cover and refrigerate for at least 6 hours.

3. Just before serving, slowly pour the ginger ale down the side of the punch bowl. Stir gently. Serve the punch in tall glasses garnished with peach slices and nasturtiums.

CHOCOLATE MINT CREAM

SERVES 6

¼ cup loosely packed fresh mint,
   or I mint tea bag
I cup milk or half-and-half
½ cup chocolate syrup

I (I-liter) bottle cold
   sparkling water
6 mint sprigs, for garnish

1. Place the mint or tea bag in a small teapot or bowl. Pour ½ cup boiling water over it. Cover and steep until cool. Strain.

2. In a pitcher, mix the milk or half-and-half and chocolate syrup.

3. Gradually whisk in the tea.

4. For each serving, pour about ⅓ cup of the chocolate mixture into a glass over ice cubes and add about ⅔ cup sparkling water. Stir, then garnish with mint sprigs.

Celebration Fare

*O*pen your doors and let the party begin. Sharing food was surely one of the earliest social activities. And in 1665, Samuel Pepys observed, "Strange to see how a good dinner and feasting reconciles everybody" ~ an observation that would hold as true today. Here we offer food and drink to suit many an occasion, but before you agonize over your menu, remember that for your guests, the mere fact of being invited is a salve to the soul.

CINNAMON ALMONDS

MAKES 11 TO 12 CUPS

4 egg whites
½ cup Champagne, preferably brut
2 cups sugar

2 teaspoons salt
I tablespoon ground cinnamon
8 cups almonds

1. Preheat the oven to 250°F. Spray two 15 by 10 by 2-inch baking pans with nonstick coating.

2. Whisk the egg whites in a large bowl until lightly beaten. Add the Champagne, sugar, and salt. Whisk until blended. Add the cinnamon and almonds. Stir until the almonds are coated. Spread the nuts in the prepared pans.

3. Bake for I to 1¼ hours, until the coating is absorbed and the almonds appear dry. Stir them occasionally to prevent sticking.

4. Line two racks with waxed paper. Remove the nuts from the pans at once and cool them on the racks,

separating the nuts with two forks.

5. Store at room temperature in an airtight container for a day or two.

VARIATIONS

For Gingered Pecans, use 2 teaspoons cinnamon and I teaspoon ground ginger in place of the cinnamon. Use 8 cups pecan halves in place of the almonds.

For Five-Spice Walnuts, use I teaspoon cinnamon, I teaspoon ground nutmeg, ½ teaspoon ground ginger, ¼ teaspoon ground cloves, and ¼ teaspoon ground allspice in place of the cinnamon. Use 8 cups walnut halves in place of the almonds.

*On a formal table,
a thoughtful hostess might
include a written
menu for the evening's meal,
placed in a pretty holder
or just nestled between the
dishes at each place
setting. It's a custom worth
considering.*

VEGETABLE TERRINE

SERVES 8

VEGETABLE LAYERS

1¾ ounces dried shiitake mushrooms

6 to 7 large cabbage leaves (preferably savoy)

1 bunch (12 ounces) spinach, stemmed

12 ounces fresh asparagus, trimmed and peeled

2 red bell peppers, cut in strips

¾ pound carrots, cut in julienne

1 (14½-ounce) can artichoke hearts, drained and quartered lengthwise

BATTER

4 eggs

½ cup buttermilk

1 tablespoon chopped parsley

1 teaspoon dried thyme

1 teaspoon dried tarragon

2 shallots, chopped

Salt and pepper to taste

TOMATO SAUCE

1 large tomato, peeled, seeded, and chopped

¼ cup buttermilk

1 tablespoon tomato paste

Pinch of cayenne

1 garlic clove, chopped

Salt and pepper to taste

1. To make the vegetable layers, pour hot water to cover the mushrooms in a small bowl and let stand for 30 minutes. Drain.

2. Meanwhile, bring a large pot of water to a boil. Blanch the cabbage leaves for 3 minutes. Plunge the leaves into ice water and drain. In the same water, blanch the spinach leaves 1 minute, then the asparagus 3 minutes, the red pepper 3 minutes, and the carrots 4 minutes. Plunge each vegetable into ice water after blanching and drain.

3. Pat dry all the blanched vegetables, the mushrooms, and the artichokes with paper towels, pressing gently to extract as much liquid as possible. (The spinach leaves should be spread out flat to their original shape.)

4. To make the batter, combine the eggs, ½ cup buttermilk, and the parsley, thyme, tarragon, and shallots in a bowl. Whisk until blended. Season liberally with salt and pepper because this will flavor all the vegetables in the terrine.

5. Generously butter a 9 by 5 by 3-inch loaf pan.

6. Using a triangle-shaped cut, remove 1 to 2 inches of hard white stem end from each cabbage leaf to make the leaves more flexible. Line the sides, then the bottom, of the pan with cabbage leaves, overlapping the leaves generously to form a leakproof shell and allowing the leaves to extend well over the rim of the pan. Pour ½ cup of the batter into the pan.

7. Arrange the asparagus spears lengthwise in the pan, packing them tightly. Top with two layers of red pepper strips placed crosswise.

Pour in a little more batter, pressing the peppers down gently. (Pressing down each layer will raise the level of the batter.)

8. Layer the mushrooms over the peppers and press gently. Layer the carrots lengthwise in the pan. Pour in a little more batter, pressing the carrots down gently.

9. Layer half the spinach leaves over the carrots. Add a layer of artichoke hearts over the spinach, then a little more batter. Gently press down the artichoke hearts.

10. Top with the remaining spinach leaves and then the remaining batter, pressing down each layer. Fold the ends of the cabbage leaves over the top of the terrine.

11. Preheat the oven to 350°F. Cover the loaf pan with buttered parchment paper cut to fit the inside edges of the pan. Place the loaf pan in a 13 by 9 by 2-inch baking pan. Pour hot water around the loaf pan to a depth of 1 inch.

12. Bake for 2 hours, or until firm. Remove the loaf pan from the water bath but do not uncover. Cool on a rack for 2 hours and refrigerate overnight.

13. To make the tomato sauce, combine the tomato, ¼ cup buttermilk, tomato paste, cayenne, and garlic in a blender. Season with salt and pepper. Blend until smooth.

14. Loosen the edges of the terrine with a knife. Invert the terrine onto a platter or cutting board. Slice it with a serrated knife. Spread tomato sauce on each plate and arrange a slice of terrine over the sauce.

SMOKED SALMON CANAPÉS

MAKES 1 DOZEN

The trick to canapés is making them both look and taste appealing. This simple recipe accomplishes that goal with the help of the tobiko, bright orange flying-fish roe. It can be found at Japanese markets, or you can substitute Canadian golden caviar.

6 slices dark rye cocktail bread

2 ounces thinly sliced smoked salmon

2 (3-ounce) packages cream cheese with chives, softened

Tobiko and dill sprigs, for garnish

1. Cut each slice of bread in half diagonally. Top each half with a thin strip of smoked salmon.

2. Pipe a rosette of chive cream cheese on the salmon. Garnish each canapé with a very small spoonful of the tobiko and a sprig of dill.

Menus to Remember

COCKTAIL PARTY

Camembert with Wine & Pistachio Nuts

MAKES 1 CUP

1 (4½-ounce) wheel underripe
  Camembert, chilled

Dry white wine

½ cup (1 stick) unsalted butter,
  softened

1 tablespoon brandy

⅛ teaspoon salt

⅛ teaspoon cayenne

¼ cup chopped natural
  pistachio nuts

1. Cut the rind from the Camembert. Reserve the container. Quarter the cheese and place it in a glass or ceramic bowl. Add enough wine to cover the cheese, then cover the bowl and marinate at room temperature for 12 hours or overnight.

2. Transfer the cheese quarters to paper towels. Pat dry the top and side of the cheese. Reserve the marinating liquid.

3. In a medium-size bowl, mash together the cheese and softened butter with a fork, adding about 2 teaspoons of the marinating liquid to moisten the mixture. Stir with a wooden spoon until well blended.

4. Season the mixture with brandy, salt and cayenne.

5. Line the Camembert container with foil or plastic wrap. Spoon half of the cheese mixture into the container and top with half of the nuts. Pile the rest of the cheese mixture on top. With a spatula, spread the cheese into an even layer.

6. Cover and chill until the cheese is firm, about 3 hours.

7. Finely chop the remaining pistachio nuts and spread them on a plate. Unwrap the cheese and roll the edges in the nuts. Allow the cheese to soften for 1 hour. Serve with crackers.

Strawberry Cream Cheese

MAKES 3 1/4 CUPS

For the pure of heart, make this cheese in small, individual heart molds. Turn each out onto a heart-shaped cracker or bread that has been cut with a heart-shaped cookie cutter. Top with three currants and a mint leaf or two.

1 envelope unflavored gelatin

½ cup sugar

1 cup sliced strawberries

2 tablespoons strawberry liqueur

2 (8-ounce) packages cream
  cheese, cut up and softened

Currants and mint sprigs,
  for garnish

1. Oil one large or several small heart-shaped molds.
2. In the large bowl of an electric mixer, thoroughly combine the gelatin and sugar.
3. Mash the strawberries in a small saucepan. Add ¾ cup of water. Bring to a boil, reduce the heat, cover, and simmer for 5 minutes.
4. Press the strawberries through a fine sieve. Reserve the juice and discard the pulp.

5. Bring 1 cup of the juice to a boil and add it to the gelatin and sugar. Stir until the gelatin dissolves. Stir in the liqueur. Add the cream cheese and beat at low speed to blend, then at medium speed until smooth.
6. Pour the cheese mixture into the prepared molds. Refrigerate for 3 to 4 hours, until firm. Unmold the cheese and garnish with currants and mint.

STILTON CHEESE SPREAD WITH SLICED PEARS

MAKES 3 CUPS

The blue-veined Stilton is a cow's milk cheese strong in flavor and regal in heritage, known as the king of English cheeses. It is named for the English village where it first was sold.

1½ (8-ounce) packages cream cheese, softened and cut up

½ cup (1 stick) unsalted butter, softened and cut up

8 ounces Stilton, softened

½ cup chopped toasted walnuts

2 pears, peeled, cored, and sliced

1. Line a 7-inch springform pan with plastic wrap.
2. In the bowl of a food processor, combine the cream cheese and butter. Pulse with on/off turns until blended. Crumble the Stilton into the bowl and pulse until mixed.
3. Press the cheese mixture evenly into the prepared pan. Cover and refrigerate the mixture until it is firm, about 3 hours.

4. To serve, remove the side from the pan. Invert the cheese onto a plate. Remove the bottom from the pan and peel off the plastic wrap. Invert the cheese onto a large serving plate and allow it to sit at room temperature for 1 hour. Smooth any cracks in the mold with a wet knife. Sprinkle the cheese with walnuts and surround it with crackers and pear slices.

149

NAPKIN
RINGS

*Whether of wicker,
ceramic, silver, or gold, napkin
rings today give spirit and
order to a table and certainly
are a sign of a special
meal. That was not always
so. Originally a Victorian
device spurred on by
the popularity of silverplate,
napkin rings enabled
diners to identify their napkins,
which were reused over
several meals because linens
could not be washed for
each. Despite their utility,
napkins rings were
produced in myriad designs ~
flora and fauna, girls
in frilly bonnets, monograms,
and more.*

PORT-CHEDDAR SPREAD

MAKES 3 1/2 CUPS

I (15¼-ounce) can crushed
  pineapple

I (8-ounce) package cream
  cheese, softened

2 cups (8 ounces) shredded
  cheddar cheese

⅓ cup port wine

I teaspoon seasoned salt

¼ to ½ teaspoon garlic powder

¼ teaspoon dry mustard

2 tablespoons minced parsley

Radicchio leaves and cucumber
  strips, for garnish

I. Lightly oil a 3½-cup mold. Drain the pineapple thoroughly in a sieve, gently pressing out as much liquid as possible.

2. In the small bowl of an electric mixer, beat the cheeses and wine at medium speed until blended. Beat in the seasoned salt, garlic powder, and dry mustard. Fold in the parsley and the drained pineapple.

3. Pack the cheese mixture into the prepared mold. Cover and refrigerate at least 4 hours or overnight.

4. Unmold the cheese onto a serving platter lined with radicchio leaves and garnish with a strip of cucumber rolled up and set on its edge to resemble a flower.

TRIO OF CHEESY PARCELS

SERVES 4

4 ounces Brie

4 ounces Roquefort (not blue
  cheese)

4 ounces Boursin

4 sheets phyllo pastry,
  thawed if frozen

4 tablespoons butter, melted

⅔ cup canned whole cranberry
  sauce

2 tablespoons port wine

Dill sprigs, for garnish

I. Preheat the oven to 425°F.

2. Divide each type of cheese into four equal pieces: Shape the Brie into balls with the rind toward the outside of the ball. Cut the Roquefort into 4 large cubes. Roll the Boursin into balls.

3. Freeze the cheeses for about 10 minutes while preparing the pastry.

4. Keep the phyllo pastry you are not working with covered with a damp tea towel. Brush I sheet of phyllo pastry with melted butter. Top with a second sheet of pastry. Cut the pastry in half lengthwise, then cut each long strip into 3 equal pieces, making 6 squares in all. Cover with a damp towel.

5. Repeat with the remaining 2 sheets of pastry and the remaining melted butter.

6. Working with 2 squares at a

time, brush the pastry with melted butter. Keep the remaining squares covered with a damp tea towel.

7. Center 1 ball of cheese on each pastry square. (Place the Brie with its rind down.) Fold the pastry corners into the center and lightly twist together to seal. Pinch together all the edges to seal. Brush with melted butter. Repeat with the remaining pastry and cheese.

8. Arrange the parcels in three groups, according to cheese filling, on an unbuttered baking sheet.

9. Bake the pastries for 12 minutes, or until browned and crispy.

10. Meanwhile, combine the cranberry sauce and port in a heavy small saucepan. Bring to a boil, stirring, over medium-high heat.

11. Pour the cranberry sauce on four plates. Arrange a hot parcel with each type of cheese filling on each plate. Garnish with dill.

RICOTTA-STUFFED SQUASH BLOSSOMS

MAKES 15 TO 25

1 (15-ounce) carton ricotta

½ cup finely chopped onion

½ cup toasted almonds, finely chopped

½ cup freshly grated Asiago or Parmesan

2 tablespoons minced fresh basil, or 2 teaspoons dried

2 tablespoons minced fresh parsley

1 teaspoon seasoned salt

½ teaspoon pepper

15 to 25 pesticide-free squash blossoms

2 tablespoons unsalted butter, melted

1. In a medium-size bowl, mix together the ricotta cheese, onion, almonds, Asiago, basil, parsley, seasoned salt, and pepper. Stir to combine the ingredients.

2. Preheat the oven to 350°F.

3. Spoon 1½ to 2½ tablespoons of the filling into each squash blossom, depending on its size. Be careful not to overfill. Gently fold the blossom ends over the filling. Arrange them in a shallow baking dish. Drizzle with the melted butter.

4. Bake for 15 minutes, or until the filling is heated through.

VARIATIONS

For Ricotta-Stuffed Mushrooms, use 20 large mushroom caps. Mound 2 tablespoons of filling in each mushroom. Brush with melted butter and bake as above.

For Ricotta-Stuffed Pea Pods, use 40 large Chinese pea pods. Stem and string the pea pods. Starting at the flat side, split the pea pods lengthwise, forming pockets. Spoon 1 tablespoon of the filling into each pod. Brush the pods with melted butter. Arrange in a shallow baking dish and bake for 10 minutes.

CHÈVRE WALNUT WAFERS

MAKES 3 DOZEN

Distinctive, tart chèvre, made from the milk of goats, usually is aged only a month or so. This versatile cheese comes in logs, cones, and spheres; it is dusted with spices or wood ash and used for slicing, spreading, or crumbling.

4 ounces aged chèvre such as Bucheron, crumbled (1 cup)

½ cup (1 stick) cold unsalted butter, cut in small pieces

1 cup all-purpose flour

1 teaspoon thyme leaves

¼ teaspoon cayenne

⅛ teaspoon salt

⅓ cup finely chopped walnuts

36 walnut halves, for garnish

1. In the bowl of a food processor, combine the chèvre, butter, flour, thyme, cayenne, and salt. Process until the dough forms a ball.
2. Turn the dough into a bowl. Stir in the chopped walnuts. Using your hands, form the dough into a log 9 inches long and 1½ inches in diameter. Wrap in plastic wrap and refrigerate for at least 1 hour.

3. Preheat the oven to 375°F.
4. Slice the dough into ¼-inch-thick wafers. Arrange the slices 1 inch apart on two unbuttered baking sheets. Place a walnut half in the center of each wafer.
5. Bake for 10 to 12 minutes, until the wafers are golden brown. Remove the wafers from the baking sheet and cool on a rack.

PISTACHIO NUT BREAD TWISTS

MAKES 2 DOZEN

½ (17¼-ounce) package frozen puff pastry, thawed (1 sheet)

2 tablespoons unsalted butter, melted

¼ cup finely chopped natural pistachio nuts

½ to 1 teaspoon cayenne or paprika

2 tablespoons grated Parmesan

1. Preheat the oven to 450°F. Butter two baking sheets.
2. Unfold the pastry on a lightly floured board. Roll it out to a 12-inch square, trimming to make the edges even. Brush the pastry with 1 tablespoon of the melted butter. Spread half the pastry with the nuts and sprinkle with the cayenne or paprika.

3. Fold the dough in half, enclosing the filling, and pat firmly together. Brush the top with the remaining butter. Sprinkle evenly with the Parmesan.

4. Cut the pastry crosswise into ½-inch-wide strips. Twist the strips into spirals as you place them, 1 inch apart, on the baking sheets.

5. Bake the twists for 8 to 10 minutes, until they are golden brown. Remove the twists from the sheets and cool them on wire racks.

Mushroom Strudel

SERVES 8

Greek phyllo pastry, available fresh or frozen at many markets, is thin as tissue and enables the baker to turn out delicate pastries like this one. Phyllo is a cousin to Germany's hand-stretched strudel dough. Both dry out and become brittle very quickly, so be sure to keep a slightly damp tea towel over the sheets: It is impossible to roll a strudel unless the dough is pliable.

8 ounces fresh mushrooms, chopped

3 tablespoons unsalted butter, plus 3 tablespoons melted

1 garlic clove, crushed

2 tablespoons dry sherry

2 tablespoons chopped parsley

2 tablespoons chopped scallions

Salt and pepper to taste

¼ cup sour cream

1 cup seasoned fine dry bread crumbs

3 sheets phyllo pastry, thawed if frozen

2 tablespoons grated Parmesan

1. Press the mushrooms between paper towels to extract the moisture. Melt 3 tablespoons of the butter in a skillet, and sauté the mushrooms and garlic for 5 minutes.

2. Add the sherry, parsley, and scallions, and season with salt and pepper. Cook until most of the liquid evaporates, then remove the pan from the heat. Stir in the sour cream and the bread crumbs. (The filling will be dry.)

3. Keep the phyllo pastry you are not working with covered with a damp tea towel. Lay 1 sheet on the counter with the short side toward the edge. Brush with some of the melted butter and sprinkle with a third of the Parmesan. Repeat with the remaining 2 sheets of pastry, melted butter, and Parmesan.

4. Spread the mushroom filling along the short side of the dough nearest the counter edge, leaving a

GIVE IT A SWIRL

You can give a soup or sauce a professional touch with a swirl in a contrasting color. In the soup, the swirl is made from crème frâiche or sour cream, but you could use a puree of peppers or any thick liquid of a complementary flavor. It's a simple technique, but it takes some practice. Gently drop a small amount of cream on the surface of the soup, then, using a skewer or a knife, drag the tip through the cream to make whatever design you choose. You can make a sunburst by squeezing the cream through a plastic bottle in a circle. Then use the knife or skewer to drag the cream outward to a point at even intervals around the circle.

I-inch border at the bottom, a ½-inch border along both sides, and a 2-inch border at the top.

5. Roll the pastry, jelly-roll fashion, starting at the short side, until the roll is 2 inches from the end. Brush the end with butter and finish rolling the dough. Place the strudel on a baking sheet. Brush the top and sides with butter.

6. Refrigerate the strudel until it is firm, about 1½ to 2 hours.

7. Preheat the oven to 450°F.

8. On the baking sheet, cut the strudel into 8 slices, keeping the slices intact to form the same roll shape. Bake for 15 to 20 minutes, until golden brown.

Squash Soup

SERVES 6 TO 8

4 pounds assorted winter squash such as acorn, butternut, or delicata

4 tablespoons unsalted butter

2 medium-size onions, halved and thinly sliced

¼ cup Champagne, preferably blanc de blancs

4 to 5 cups chicken stock

I teaspoon freshly grated nutmeg

Salt and white pepper to taste

Crème Fraîche (page 187) or sour cream, for garnish

1. Preheat the oven to 325°F. Line a baking sheet with foil.

2. Quarter the squash and scoop out the seeds. Place the quarters skin side up on the baking sheet.

3. Bake for 1 to 1½ hours, until the squash is tender. Cool. Scoop out the pulp and puree it in several batches in a food processor.

4. In a heavy large skillet, melt 2 tablespoons of the butter and sauté the onions until translucent. Add the Champagne and cook for 15 minutes, until the liquid is absorbed and the onions are golden brown, stirring often. Puree the onions with a little of the squash in a food processor.

5. Combine the onion and squash purees in a large saucepan. Whisk in the chicken stock until the soup is the desired consistency. Cover and heat through over medium heat, stirring occasionally.

6. Whisk in the remaining 2 tablespoons of butter. Season with the nutmeg and salt and pepper.

7. Ladle the soup into bowls. Swirl crème fraîche on each serving.

SCALLION FANS

A scallion fan, or brush, gives a touch of crispness to Scalloped Oysters or any dish on a buffet table. And it's simple to make. Cut the root end of a scallion just above the root, so the layers are no longer held together. Cut the scallion top so you are left with a 3-inch-long piece. Then, at each end, make several inch-long slices so there are many slender strips held together in the center. Drop the fan into a bowl of ice water for an hour or so, and the strips will spread out.

SCALLOPED OYSTERS

SERVES 4

"Roystering" is a term the Victorians coined for the raucous merriment that accompanied feasts where oysters were served. Fred Parks of Parks' Seafood in Allentown, Pennsylvania, says his restaurant is a shrine to oysters and the oyster craze that gripped the United States in the 1880s. Naturally, roystering is among his favorite activities. Oysters and Champagne are a classic New Year's Day combination.

30 shucked oysters, with their liquor
Milk
¼ teaspoon Worcestershire sauce
½ cup (1 stick) unsalted butter
½ teaspoon finely grated onion

½ teaspoon celery salt
⅛ teaspoon pepper
2 cups coarse saltine cracker crumbs
Scallion fans, for garnish (see sidebar, left)

1. Preheat the oven to 350°F. Butter an 8-inch round cake dish.
2. Drain the oysters, reserving their liquor. Add enough milk to the liquor to make 1 cup. Stir in the Worcestershire sauce.
3. In a medium-size skillet, melt the butter and sauté the onion until it is translucent. Remove the onion from the heat and season it with the celery salt and pepper. Add the cracker crumbs, tossing to coat them.
4. Sprinkle one third of the crumb mixture on the bottom of the prepared dish. Layer with half the oysters. Repeat the layers, ending with a layer of crumbs. Pour the milk mixture over the casserole.
5. Bake for 35 to 45 minutes, until the crumbs are brown and the center is hot. Garnish with scallion fans.

ROASTED MARYLAND CRAB CAKES

SERVES 5

Chef Etienne Jaulin's specialties at the Old Angler's Inn in Potomac, Maryland, owe their distinctive flavor to fresh local ingredients. Much of the fish and seafood is caught nearby in Chesapeake Bay, but any fresh crab can be used.

1 pound jumbo lump
    crabmeat

2 medium-size tomatoes,
    peeled and seeded

8 ounces scallops

½ cup heavy cream

Salt and pepper to taste

1 bunch scallions,
    thinly sliced

RED PEPPER COULIS

2 large red bell peppers

1 cup heavy cream

YELLOW PEPPER COULIS

2 large yellow bell peppers

1 cup heavy cream

Sage sprigs, for garnish

1. Pick through the crabmeat to remove any shells. Cut the outer tomato flesh in julienne and pat dry on paper towels.

2. In the bowl of a food processor, puree the scallops. With the food processor running, quickly add the ½ cup cream and process just until blended. Season with salt and pepper.

3. In a large bowl, combine the crab, tomato, scallop puree, and scallions. Mix well. Cover and refrigerate for at least 2 hours.

4. Make each coulis separately. Remove the stem, seeds, and membrane from the peppers. Cut the peppers into chunks. In a medium-size saucepan, combine the peppers and the 1 cup cream. Bring to a simmer. Reduce the heat. Cover and cook, barely simmering, for 30 minutes. Puree the mixture in a food processor. Pour through a sieve and keep the coulis warm.

5. Preheat the oven to 425°F. Butter a 15 by 10 by 1-inch nonstick baking pan.

6. Spoon 5 rounded mounds of crab mixture onto the pan, using about ¾ cup for each cake. Bake for 20 to 25 minutes, until heated through and set in the center.

7. Arrange the red pepper coulis and yellow pepper coulis in pools on each plate so that the two sauces meet but do not mix. Place a cake on top, in the center of the plate. Garnish with sage sprigs.

Glazed Baked Ham with Orange Madeira Sauce

SERVES 10 TO 14

BAKED HAM

1 (10- to 14-pound) bone-in, fully cooked smoked ham

3 to 4 cups cider

BRANDIED FRUIT

Fresh fruit such as apricots, peaches, melons, cherries, pineapple, and pears (enough to make 3 cups of sliced fruit)

¾ cup cider

¾ cup brandy

HONEY APRICOT GLAZE

¼ cup apricot preserves

¼ cup orange marmalade

2 tablespoons honey

1 teaspoon dry mustard

½ teaspoon ground ginger

ORANGE MADEIRA SAUCE

4 cups beef bouillon

¾ cup Madeira

Zest of 1 orange

3 tablespoons cold unsalted butter, cut in 12 pieces

1. Preheat the oven to 325°F.

2. To bake the ham, place it, fat side up, on a rack in a shallow roasting pan. Pour cider over the ham to almost touch the bottom of the ham.

3. Bake for 2½ to 3 hours, until a meat thermometer inserted in the thickest part registers 130°F. Baste the ham with pan juices several times during baking. Add more cider, if necessary, to keep some liquid in the bottom of the pan. If the ham starts to turn too brown, cover it with foil.

4. While the ham bakes, make the brandied fruit: Peel and slice, halve, or quarter 3 cups of fruit and put it in a deep bowl. Combine ¾ cup cider and the brandy, and pour over the fruit (there should be enough to cover the fruit). Cover the bowl and let it stand for 1 to 2 hours. Drain.

5. To make the glaze, mix the apricot preserves, orange marmalade, and honey in a small bowl. Sprinkle in the dry mustard and then the ginger, mixing well after each.

6. To make the sauce, combine the bouillon, Madeira, and orange zest in a heavy large saucepan. Boil the liquid gently until it is reduced to 3 cups. Remove from the heat and discard the orange zest.

7. Whisk in the butter, 1 piece at a time, until it is melted. Cover the saucepan to keep the sauce warm.

8. When the meat thermometer inserted in the ham registers 130°F (see Step 3), brush the ham liberally with the glaze. Bake the ham for an additional 15 minutes.

9. Arrange the brandied fruit decoratively on the ham, securing the fruit with wooden toothpicks. Brush the fruit and the ham with more glaze. Bake the ham 15 minutes longer.

10. Let the ham stand for 10 minutes before carving. Serve it with the sauce.

ROAST TURKEY WITH CHESTNUT SAUCE

SERVES 8

I (12- to 14-pound) turkey (reserve liver and heart)

Salt and pepper to taste

Sausage Stuffing for Turkey (opposite)

5 soaked morel mushrooms (reserved from Sausage Stuffing recipe)

10 small parsley sprigs

14 tablespoons (1¾ sticks) unsalted butter, softened, plus additional for basting

I or 2 Delicious apples, red or golden, cored and sliced

4 ounces large, fresh mushrooms, cut in thick slices

I medium-size onion, sliced

I pound cooked chestnuts or 2 (8-ounce) jars whole chestnuts, drained

¼ cup apple brandy, such as Calvados

I to 2 teaspoons dark cocoa powder

1. Preheat the oven to 325°F.

2. Rinse the turkey and pat it dry, inside and out, with paper towels. Season with salt and pepper. Fill the bird with stuffing, truss it, and place it in a shallow roasting pan.

3. With your fingers, release the skin from the breast and upper leg. Place the reserved morels and the parsley sprigs between the skin and meat. (As the turkey cooks, the parsley and morels will show through the skin as well as add flavor.)

4. Rub the outside of the bird with ½ cup of the butter. Place the turkey in the oven and baste it often, adding more butter if necessary so there is sufficient juice in the bottom of the pan for basting.

5. Meanwhile, melt 2 tablespoons of the butter in a skillet and sauté the apples until crisp-tender. Drain. Melt 2 more tablespoons of the butter in the skillet and sauté the fresh mushrooms briefly, until golden. Drain. Melt the remaining 2 tablespoons of butter and sauté the onion until tender.

6. After the turkey has cooked 3½ to 4 hours, a meat thermometer inserted between the leg and thigh should register 165° to 170°F. Remove the turkey from the oven. Place the apple and fresh mushroom slices alternately down the upper side of the bird. Secure them in place with wooden toothpicks.

7. Roast the turkey an additional 30 minutes, or until a meat thermometer inserted between the leg and thigh registers 180° to 185°F, the leg feels loose at the joint, and the center of the stuffing registers 165°F. Transfer the turkey to a large, warm platter. Cover it loosely with foil to keep it warm, and let it sit for 20 minutes to let the juices settle.

8. Pour the drippings from the roasting pan into a medium-size bowl. Spoon the fat from the top and discard it.

9. In a food processor or blender, combine ½ cup of the pan juices with the onion, chestnuts, apple brandy, and cocoa. Blend until smooth. Add more pan juices to adjust the consistency as desired. Strain to remove any lumps.

10. To carve the turkey, cut off the legs and separate the thigh from the

drumstick at the joint. Slice the dark meat. Slice the breast straight down in thin, even slices.

11. To serve, place a small amount of chestnut sauce on a warm plate and top with slices of turkey. Gar-nish with apple and mushroom slices. Serve the stuffing on the side.

NOTE: As the stuffing cools, it will become firm and have a pâté-like consistency. It's delicious the next day.

Sausage Stuffing for Turkey

MAKES 5 CUPS

The Victorians called stuffing forcemeat, an odd word but certainly an appropriate one. Wait until the last minute to stuff the bird. When the bird is cooked, the temperature in the center of the stuffing must register 165°F. It is best to remove all the stuffing from the cavity right away.

I ounce dried morel mushrooms, rinsed

½ cup dry white wine

3 slices bacon, finely chopped

I turkey liver, diced

I turkey heart, diced

I medium-size onion, chopped

2 tablespoons apple brandy, such as Calvados

I pound bulk pork sausage

I pound ground veal

2 slices bread, made into soft crumbs

¾ cup chopped parsley

2 eggs

I tablespoon grated Parmesan

I teaspoon dried marjoram

I teaspoon dried oregano

I teaspoon dried rosemary

I teaspoon dried sage

I teaspoon dried thyme

½ teaspoon salt

¼ teaspoon white pepper

2 garlic cloves, finely chopped

1. In a small bowl, soak the morels in enough wine to cover for 10 minutes. Reserve 5 morels for the turkey. Chop the rest and strain the soaking liquid.

2. In a large skillet, cook the bacon until the fat is rendered and the bacon starts to brown. Add the liver and heart. Sauté until the meats are browned, stirring often. Remove them with a slotted spoon and drain them on paper towels.

3. Add the onion to the skillet and sauté until tender. Stir in the bacon mixture, apple brandy, morels, and 2 to 4 tablespoons of the strained morel liquid. Cool the mixture.

4. In a large bowl, mix the sausage, veal, bread crumbs, parsley, eggs, Parmesan, herbs, salt, pepper, and garlic. Add the bacon mixture. Mix thoroughly.

5. Use as directed in Roast Turkey (opposite).

Roast Topside of Beef

SERVES 6 TO 8

Serve this for a fall dinner with roasted onions, runner beans cooked al dente, and braised leeks tossed in butter with plenty of freshly ground black pepper.

1 (3-pound) boneless beef round tip roast (cap removed) or sirloin tip roast

Salt and pepper to taste

¼ teaspoon ground allspice

1 garlic clove, crushed

⅔ cup medium-dry cider

Juice of 1 lemon

2 tablespoons grapeseed or vegetable oil

1¼ cups beef stock

2 tablespoons unsalted butter

1 shallot, finely chopped

3 tablespoons finely chopped parsley

2 tablespoons prepared horse-radish

⅔ cup sour cream

1. Rub the meat with the salt, pepper, allspice, and garlic and place it in a large plastic bag set in a shallow baking pan. Pour the cider, lemon juice, and half the grapeseed oil over the meat. Tie the bag tightly, pressing the marinade around the meat. Refrigerate for 24 hours, turning the bag over occasionally.

2. Drain the meat, reserving the marinade in the refrigerator. Dry the meat with paper towels.

3. Preheat the oven to 350°F.

4. Heat the remaining oil in an ovenproof Dutch oven. Sear the beef well on all sides. Add the stock. Cover and bake for 1½ to 1¾ hours, until a thermometer inserted in the center of the meat registers 140°F for rare, or until done to your liking. Remove the beef from the pan, reserving the juices; keep it warm.

5. In a medium-size saucepan, melt the butter and sauté the shallot until softened. Add the cooking juices and the reserved marinade. Season lightly with salt and pepper.

6. Bring the sauce to a boil, and boil it gently until the liquid is reduced by one third. Stir in the chopped parsley.

7. While the liquid is reducing, stir the horseradish into the sour cream.

8. Slice the beef fairly thickly and pour the meat sauce over the meat slices. Serve the horseradish sauce in a small bowl.

Four-Layer Poppy Seed Torte

SERVES 10 TO 12

POPPY SEED CAKE

2½ cups cake flour

2½ teaspoons baking powder

⅔ cup unsalted butter, softened

1½ cups granulated sugar

1 cup milk

Grated zest of 1 orange

1 teaspoon vanilla extract

4 egg whites

¼ cup poppy seeds

ORANGE CREAM FILLING

1½ cups heavy cream

½ cup confectioners' sugar

½ teaspoon orange flower water or 1 tablespoon orange liqueur

Confectioners' sugar, for garnish

Pesticide-free pansies, for garnish

1. To make the cake, preheat the oven to 375°F. Butter and flour two 8-inch layer cake pans and two 9-inch layer cake pans.

2. Sift together the flour and baking powder.

3. In the large bowl of an electric mixer, cream the butter and 1¼ cups of the granulated sugar at medium speed until fluffy, scraping the side of the bowl often.

4. In a small bowl, combine the milk, orange zest, and vanilla.

5. Add the flour mixture to the butter mixture alternately with the milk mixture, beating at medium speed until blended after each addition.

6. In the small bowl of an electric mixer, using clean beaters, beat the egg whites at high speed until frothy. Gradually add the remaining granulated sugar, beating until the egg whites hold stiff peaks. Gently fold the egg whites into the batter. Fold in the poppy seeds.

7. Divide the batter among the pans and smooth the tops.

8. Bake for 15 to 18 minutes, until the cakes pull away from the sides of the pans and a cake tester inserted in the center comes out clean.

9. Cool in the pans on a rack for 15 minutes. Remove the layers from the pans and cool completely on a rack.

10. To make the filling, beat the cream in the large bowl of an electric mixer until it begins to hold its shape. Gradually add ½ cup confectioners' sugar and the orange flower water, beating to stiff peaks.

11. To assemble the cake, set one 9-inch layer on a serving plate. Spread one third of the cream filling over it. Top with the second 9-inch layer. Cover with another third of the filling and top with an 8-inch cake layer. Cover with the remaining filling and the final layer. Dust the cake generously with confectioners' sugar. Arrange a few pansies in the center of the top layer and around the cake on the plate.

bowl, cutting the cake as necessary to fit. Drizzle with 2 tablespoons orange liqueur and half the raspberry puree.

8. Spread the trifle with half the custard sauce. Add a layer of blueberries. Spread with 2 cups of the whipped cream.

9. Top with another layer of pound cake. Drizzle with the remaining orange liqueur and raspberry puree. Spread with the remaining custard sauce. Add a layer of raspberries. Spread with 1 cup whipped cream.

10. With a pastry tube, pipe the remaining whipped cream decoratively around the edge of the trifle. Cover and refrigerate for 4 to 6 hours.

ORANGE CHOCOLATE TRUFFLES

MAKES 2 DOZEN

1 cup (2 sticks) unsalted butter

1 pound semisweet chocolate, chopped

6 egg yolks

⅓ cup orange liqueur, such as Grand Marnier

Pink Roses (page 194), for garnish

1. Melt the butter in the top of a double boiler over simmering water. Add the chocolate. Stir until the chocolate is melted and smooth.

2. In a bowl, whisk the yolks. Stir a few spoonfuls of the hot chocolate mixture into the yolks. Then stir the yolk mixture into the chocolate mixture. Cook, stirring constantly, until a thermometer registers 160°F, about 4 minutes.

3. Remove the chocolate from the hot water and pour it into a bowl. Allow the mixture to cool to room temperature, stirring occasionally, for about 1 hour.

4. Gradually add the orange liqueur, whisking constantly. Cover the chocolate and refrigerate for 8 hours or overnight.

5. With cold hands, quickly roll heaping teaspoonfuls of the chocolate mixture into balls. The chocolate will be firm when you scoop it from the bowl, but it melds easily. Place the balls in paper candy cups. Decorate with the pink roses. Store them in the refrigerator.

VARIATIONS:

For some interesting variations, roll the truffles in finely chopped nuts, coconut, cocoa powder, or chocolate shavings.

FLAMING PLUM PUDDING

SERVES 12

Joy McConnell begins her plum pudding in mid-November and ages it for six weeks. She periodically adds Cognac to the cheesecloth wrapping to give it a deeper flavor. She lights it, finally, for her family at Christmas dinner.

I cup dried currants

I cup seedless raisins

I cup golden raisins

½ cup chopped candied cherries

¼ cup finely chopped candied citron

¼ cup finely chopped candied lemon peel

¼ cup finely chopped candied orange peel

I medium-size apple, chopped

I small carrot, grated

½ cup blanched slivered almonds

2 tablespoons finely chopped crystallized ginger

I cup finely ground beef suet

Juice and grated zest of I lemon

Juice and grated zest of I orange

½ cup plus 3 to 4 tablespoons Cognac

I cup all-purpose flour

½ teaspoon salt

½ teaspoon ground allspice

½ teaspoon ground cinnamon

¼ teaspoon ground nutmeg

⅛ teaspoon ground cloves

I½ cups fresh bread crumbs

6 eggs

½ cup packed light brown sugar

½ cup (I stick) unsalted butter, softened

2 cups confectioners' sugar

I teaspoon vanilla extract

¼ cup Cognac or brandy, for flaming

Tiny crabapples and sweet woodruff, for garnish

I. In a large nonreactive bowl, mix the fruits, carrot, almonds, and ginger. Stir in the suet, lemon and orange juice and zest, and ½ cup of the Cognac. Cover and refrigerate overnight or up to a week, stirring occasionally.

2. Butter and sugar a 3- to 4-quart pudding mold with a tight-fitting cover. If you don't have a mold, use a heatproof bowl.

3. Sift the flour, salt, and spices together. Sift the mixture over the fruit. Sprinkle with bread crumbs. Stir until the flour and crumbs are well distributed.

4. In the small bowl of an electric mixer, beat the eggs at high speed until they are light. Add the brown sugar and continue beating at medium speed until the mixture is thick and smooth. Pour the egg mixture over the fruit mixture and mix with a spoon until blended.

5. Spoon the pudding into the prepared mold and cover with the lid. Set the mold in a large pot on the stove. If using a bowl, cover it with heavy foil. Then drape a damp tea towel over the top and secure it with string around the rim. Draw the corners of the towel up over the bowl

DINNER BELLS

Hungry guests and eager children know to listen for the sweet summons of a dinner bell. At a formal dinner party of old, the butler might have watched the guests' progress and used a bell to let the kitchen staff know the time had come for the next course. Bells of silver, crystal, or porcelain might be chosen to complement the china, flatware, or glasses.

and tie them together. Pour boiling water in the pot to three quarters full; return it to a boil.

6. Lower the heat to maintain a gentle simmer. Cover the pot and steam the pudding for 8 hours, replenishing water as needed.

7. Cool the pudding in the covered mold set on a rack for 3 hours. Remove the lid and gently lift the pudding from the mold, loosening it with a knife around the edges. Wrap it in a heavy plastic bag and store it in refrigerator for at least 3 weeks or up to a year.

8. Before serving, cream the butter in the small bowl of an electric mixer. Beat in the confectioners' sugar until the mixture is fluffy and smooth. Add the vanilla and the remaining 3 to 4 tablespoons Cognac, beating until well blended.

9. Gently replace the pudding in a buttered and sugared mold and steam, as in Steps 5 and 6, for 2 hours.

10. Unmold and place the warm pudding on a serving dish. Pour ¼ cup warmed Cognac into a heat-proof ladle and ignite it. Pour it over the pudding and serve. Pass the sauce. Garnish with tiny crabapples and sweet woodruff.

CANADIAN WHITE FRUITCAKE

MAKES 4 LOAVES

FRUIT MIXTURE

4¾ cups (1½ pounds) coarsely chopped blanched almonds

⅔ cup (4 ounces) diced candied citron

⅔ cup (4 ounces) diced candied orange peel

⅔ cup (4 ounces) thinly sliced candied pineapple wedges

1⅓ cups (8 ounces) golden raisins

½ cup all-purpose flour

BATTER

¾ cup milk

¼ cup brandy, plus additional for soaking

1 teaspoon almond extract

1½ cups (3 sticks) unsalted butter, softened

2 cups granulated sugar

6 egg yolks

3½ cups all-purpose flour

6 egg whites

1 teaspoon cream of tartar

MARZIPAN TOPPING
(for each loaf)

1 (7-ounce) roll marzipan

CONFECTIONERS' GLAZE
(for each loaf)

1 cup confectioners' sugar

2 tablespoons unsalted butter, melted

1 tablespoon milk

½ teaspoon vanilla extract

POLISHED TO PERFECTION

Amid fancy crystal and glittering silverware, every formal table used to include knife rests, the sole task of which was to keep knife blades from soiling the tablecloth. These charming accessories were made of crystal or silver or bone, some simply elegant, some whimsically depicting a little scene.

1. To prepare the fruit, combine the almonds and fruit in a very large bowl. Sprinkle with ½ cup flour and toss to coat.

2. To make the batter, butter four 8½ by 4½ by 2½-inch loaf pans. Line the bottoms with waxed paper. Butter the waxed paper. Preheat the oven to 275°F.

3. In a small bowl, combine ¾ cup milk with the brandy and the almond extract.

4. In the large bowl of an electric mixer, beat 1½ cups butter at medium speed until creamy. Gradually add the granulated sugar, beating until light and fluffy. Add the egg yolks, one at a time, beating well after each addition.

5. Add 3½ cups flour alternately with the milk mixture, beating well after each addition. Pour the batter over the fruit mixture. Mix well.

6. Using clean beaters, in the small bowl of an electric mixer, beat the egg whites at high speed until they are foamy. Add the cream of tartar. Beat the egg whites until they form stiff peaks. Fold the egg whites into the batter.

7. Spoon the batter into the prepared pans, packing it evenly by pressing down firmly with the back of a wooden spoon.

8. Bake for 1¾ hours, until a cake tester inserted in the center comes out clean. Cool the cakes in the pans on racks for 30 minutes. Run a knife around the edges of the cakes to loosen them. Remove from the pans and peel off the waxed paper. Cool completely on a rack.

9. Soak cheesecloth in brandy, and wrap each loaf in cheesecloth and then in foil. Refrigerate the cakes for at least 2 to 3 weeks, unwrapping the foil occasionally to brush the cheesecloth with additional brandy.

10. On the day of serving, make the marzipan topping: Roll out the marzipan between two sheets of waxed paper into a rectangle the same size as the top of one cake. Remove the top sheet of waxed paper. Trim the edges of the marzipan to form an even rectangle. Invert the marzipan on top of a cake and peel off the remaining waxed paper.

11. To make the confectioners' glaze, sift the confectioners' sugar into a medium-size bowl. Stir in the melted butter, 1 tablespoon milk, and the vanilla. Mix until smooth.

12. Spread the glaze over the marzipan topping. Smooth the top of the icing with a hot knife.

CALIFORNIA FRUITCAKE

MAKES 2 LOAVES

FRUIT

I cup (6 ounces) dark raisins

⅓ cup (1¼ ounces) dried cranberries

⅓ cup (2 ounces) diced candied citron

⅓ cup (2 ounces) halved candied cherries

⅓ cup (2 ounces) diced candied lemon peel

⅓ cup (1½ ounces) chopped dried apricots

⅓ cup (2 ounces) sliced candied pineapple wedges

⅓ cup (2 ounces) diced candied orange peel

⅓ cup (1½ ounces) coarsely chopped crystallized ginger

½ cup brandy, plus additional for soaking

BATTER

1½ cups all-purpose flour

1½ teaspoons baking powder

½ teaspoon baking soda

I teaspoon ground cinnamon

½ teaspoon ground cloves

¼ teaspoon salt

¼ teaspoon ground nutmeg

½ cup (I stick) unsalted butter, softened

¾ cup packed light brown sugar

2 eggs

½ cup milk

I cup (4 ounces) chopped walnuts

½ cup (2½ ounces) chopped blanched almonds

I. To prepare the fruit, combine all the fruit and the crystallized ginger with the brandy in a large bowl. Mix well. Cover and let stand for several hours, stirring occasionally.

2. Butter two 8½ by 4½ by 2½-inch loaf pans. Line the bottoms with waxed paper and butter the waxed paper. Preheat the oven to 325°F.

3. To make the batter, sift together the flour, baking powder, baking soda, cinnamon, cloves, salt, and nutmeg into a medium-size bowl.

4. In the large bowl of an electric mixer, beat the butter at medium speed until creamy. Gradually add the brown sugar, beating until light and scraping the side of the bowl often. Add the eggs, one at a time, beating well after each addition.

5. Add the flour mixture alternately with the milk, beating at low speed until blended after each addition. Stir in the fruit mixture and nuts.

6. Spoon the batter into the prepared pans, packing it evenly by pressing down firmly with the back of a wooden spoon.

7. Bake for I hour, until a cake tester inserted in the center comes out clean. Cool the cakes in the pans set on a rack for 10 minutes. Run a knife around the edge of each cake to loosen it. Remove the cakes from the pans. Cool completely on the rack.

8. Soak cheesecloth in brandy. Wrap the cake first in cheesecloth and then in foil. Refrigerate it for at least I month, occasionally unwrapping the foil to brush the cheesecloth with more brandy.

CRANBERRY & GRAND MARNIER BOMBE IN PASTRY

SERVES 8

Phyllo pastry is one of the easiest ways to serve food *en croûte* or in a pastry crust. Here cranberries folded into homemade ice cream under the pastry shell are an unexpected touch. Plan to make this over a few days, since the ice cream needs to freeze, and the bombe needs to freeze overnight.

CRANBERRY ICE CREAM

2 (16-ounce) cans whole-berry cranberry sauce

1 teaspoon vanilla extract

2½ cups heavy cream

PHYLLO PASTRY MOLD

⅓ pound phyllo pastry (8 sheets), thawed if frozen

¼ cup unsalted butter, melted

GRAND MARNIER CREAM

½ cup sugar

1 envelope unflavored gelatin

3 egg yolks

Finely grated zest of 1 orange

½ cup orange juice

2 tablespoons Grand Marnier or other orange liqueur

1 cup heavy cream

1. To make the ice cream, puree the cranberry sauce in a food mill or processor. Strain to remove the skins and seeds, if desired. Measure 2½ cups of puree.

2. In an ice cream machine, combine the puree and vanilla with 2½ cups heavy cream. Freeze according to the manufacturer's directions. Cover; keep in the freezer at least 3 hours or until ready to use.

3. To make the pastry mold, preheat the oven to 375°F. Butter the outside of a 2-quart melon, bombe, or other freezer- and ovenproof mold.

4. Keep the phyllo pastry you are not working with covered with a damp tea towel. Spread out 1 sheet and brush well with melted butter. Continue layering with the remaining 7 sheets, brushing each with melted butter.

5. Wrap the outside of the mold with phyllo pastry, trimming the pastry to fit flush with the edge of

the mold. Make decorations by twisting strips of phyllo pastry scraps. Butter the undersides of the decorations and press them gently onto the pastry mold.

6. Place the mold, hollow side down, on a baking sheet. Bake for 20 minutes, or until golden brown.

7. Remove the mold from the oven; cool for 10 minutes. Lift the pastry off the mold. Cool it completely on a rack, hollow side down.

8. To make the Grand Marnier cream, combine the sugar and the unflavored gelatin in a small saucepan.

9. In a medium-size bowl, whisk together the egg yolks, orange zest, orange juice, and Grand Marnier until blended. Stir this into the gelatin mixture in the saucepan. Cook over medium heat for 6 to 8 minutes, whisking constantly, until the mixture thickens slightly and the gelatin dissolves.

A FRAGRANT WELCOME

One way to make holiday company feel especially welcome as they arrive is a fragrant whiff of spicy Christmas potpourri from a big bowl. Herbal decorations are also great complements to the traditional glass ornaments on the tree.

10. Cool until the mixture reaches room temperature, about 45 minutes, stirring often.

11. Whip I cup heavy cream until it holds soft peaks. Stir in the orange mixture. Refrigerate for 10 minutes, or until the mixture just begins to set up.

12. While the gelatin mixture is cooling, allow the cranberry ice cream to soften slightly. Line the inside of the mold used to make the pastry with foil, pressing it evenly into all the crevices. Spread the ice cream inside the mold, forming a shell with a hollow center. Freeze for at least 20 minutes.

13. Spoon the Grand Marnier cream into the center of the ice cream mold. Smooth the top of the ice cream and freeze until firm, 6 hours or overnight.

14. To serve, invert the mold onto a serving plate and remove the foil. Cover the ice cream with pastry. Cut at the table with a serrated knife.

FATHER CHRISTMAS SHORTBREAD

MAKES 1 TO 2 DOZEN

3 cups all-purpose flour
½ teaspoon baking powder
I cup (2 sticks) unsalted butter, softened
I cup sugar

I egg
I tablespoon vanilla extract
Candies or dried currants, for garnish

1. In a large bowl, stir together the flour and baking powder.

2. In the large bowl of an electric mixer, cream the butter and sugar at medium speed until light and fluffy, about 5 minutes. Add the egg and vanilla. Beat until blended. Gradually beat the dry ingredients into the butter mixture at low speed, mixing well after each addition and scraping the beaters frequently.

3. Turn the dough out on a lightly floured surface. Using a rubber spatula to lift and turn the dough, gently knead it until it is smooth and forms a ball. Divide the dough in half. Gather each half into a ball and wrap in plastic wrap. Refrigerate for several hours.

4. Preheat the oven to 325°F.

5. On a lightly floured surface, roll the chilled dough, I ball at a time, to a thickness of ½ inch. Cut with 2½- or 3-inch cookie cutters.

6. Put the cookies on unbuttered baking sheets. Garnish them with candies or dried currants.

7. Bake on a low rack for 20 to 25 minutes, until the cookies begin to color lightly. (They should not brown.) Cool them on a rack. Store them in airtight containers.

THE SCENTS OF CHRISTMAS

For herbalist and cook Emelie Tolley, Christmas is linked to a bouquet of scents. She suggests filling the house with holiday aromas by brewing mulled wine or cider. To a half-gallon of red wine or cider, add 2 cinnamon sticks, 10 whole cloves, 10 allspice berries, 1 dried orange peel, 10 cardamom pods, and ½ teaspoon of coriander seed. Heat it slowly and let it steep for half an hour. Serve hot.

Mascarpone Coeur à la Crème

SERVES 6

A former drama student, Patrick O'Connell is a master at wooing his audience, the guests at his Inn at Little Washington in Virginia. This rich, romantic dessert is certain to win applause.

1 (8-ounce) package mascarpone cheese or cream cheese, softened

2 tablespoons raspberry liqueur, such as Chambord

1 teaspoon lemon juice

1 teaspoon vanilla extract

1¼ cups heavy cream, plus additional for garnish

⅔ cup confectioners' sugar

Raspberry Puree (page 194)

Raspberries and mint sprigs, for garnish

1. In the small bowl of an electric mixer, combine the cheese, liqueur, lemon juice, and vanilla. Beat at medium speed just until smooth. (Overbeating the mascarpone will cause it to separate.)

2. Using clean beaters, in the large bowl of an electric mixer, beat the cream at medium speed until it barely begins to hold its shape. Gradually add the confectioners' sugar, beating to medium peaks. Gradually fold the whipped cream into the cheese mixture.

3. Line six ½-cup heart-shaped molds with drainage holes with double layers of damp cheesecloth. Divide the cheese mixture among the molds, spreading evenly. Wrap cheesecloth over the cheese mixture. Put the molds on a tray and refrigerate for at least 2 hours.

4. To serve, unfold the cheesecloth from the top of the molds. Invert each mold onto a serving plate and remove the cheesecloth. Spoon raspberry puree around the cheese hearts and garnish with raspberries and mint sprigs.

5. To make little hearts, pour 3 large drops of heavy cream onto the sauce, about half an inch apart along one side of each dessert. Draw the tip of a paring knife through each drop of cream to form the crevice and point of a heart.

CHOCOLATE HAZELNUT HEART CAKE

SERVES 8

12 ounces semisweet chocolate, chopped

5 egg yolks

12 tablespoons ground hazelnuts

4 tablespoons plain dry bread crumbs

6 egg whites

½ cup sugar

1 cup heavy cream

¼ cup raspberry jam

Chocolate curls, silver dragées, and Pink Roses (page 194), for garnish

1. Butter and flour two 8-inch heart-shaped or round layer cake pans. Line them with waxed paper and butter and flour the paper.

2. Melt 4 ounces of the chocolate in the top of a double boiler over simmering water. Remove the chocolate from the hot water and whisk in the egg yolks, one at a time. Stir in 6 tablespoons of the nuts and 2 tablespoons of the bread crumbs.

3. Preheat the oven to 375°F.

4. In the large bowl of an electric mixer, beat the egg whites until soft peaks form. Gradually add the sugar, beating until the egg whites are stiff and shiny.

5. Fold a few spoonfuls of egg white into the chocolate mixture. Gradually fold the chocolate mixture into the remaining whites. Fold in the remaining 6 tablespoons of hazelnuts and 2 tablespoons of bread crumbs. Spread the batter in the prepared pans.

6. Bake for 25 to 30 minutes, until the cakes pull away from the sides of the pans and a cake tester inserted in the center comes out clean. (The cakes will rise in the pan, then settle during baking.)

7. Cool the cakes completely in the pans set on racks. Carefully remove the cakes from the pans. Peel away the waxed paper.

8. In a heavy small saucepan, heat the cream over medium-low heat until hot. Add the remaining 8 ounces of chocolate. Whisk the ganache constantly until the chocolate is melted. Do not boil.

9. Brush loose crumbs from the cake layers. Place one layer on a rack set on a baking sheet. Spread the raspberry jam on top, then drizzle evenly with a third of the warm ganache. Add the top cake layer. Drizzle a third of the warm ganache evenly over the top of the cake, forming a mirror-like finish. Refrigerate to set the glaze.

10. Cover and refrigerate the remaining ganache for 2 hours, until it reaches spreading consistency.

11. Transfer the cake to a serving plate. Spread a thin layer of chilled ganache on the sides of the cake, then gently press on chocolate curls.

12. With a pastry tube, pipe a ganache border on the cake. Garnish with chocolate curls and silver dragées. Garnish the center of the cake with pink roses. Refrigerate until an hour before serving.

CLARET CUP

MAKES 8 CUPS

The poet John Keats took to claret (the English name for red Bordeaux wine) with great affection, writing to his brother: "It fills one's mouth with a gushing freshness, then goes down cool and feverless . . . as fragrant as the Queen Bee."

⅔ cup sugar

2 large oranges, sliced

6 whole cloves

2 cinnamon sticks

2 whole nutmegs

5 cups good-quality red Bordeaux

¼ cup brandy

2 tablespoons orange liqueur

1. In a large saucepan, combine 2½ cups of water with the sugar and orange slices.
2. Tie the cloves, cinnamon sticks, and nutmegs in cheesecloth. Add the bundle to the orange mixture.
3. Bring to a boil, stirring to dissolve the sugar. Remove the orange mixture from the heat, cover, and let steep for 1 hour.
4. Stir in the Bordeaux, brandy, and orange liqueur. Heat through.
5. Remove the spices. Serve warm in claret cups or wine glasses.

HUNSTRETE HOUSE CHRISTMAS PUNCH

MAKES 3 1/2 CUPS

¼ cup sugar

4 lemons, sliced

2 oranges, sliced

2 teaspoons whole cloves

1½ cups Southern Comfort

1½ cups Canadian whisky

¾ cup white rum

Cinnamon sticks, lemon twists, and whole cloves, for garnish

1. In a sterilized 2-quart jar, combine the sugar, lemon and orange slices, cloves, Southern Comfort, whisky, and rum. Mix well, immersing the fruit as much as possible.
2. Seal the jar and refrigerate the punch for 1 month.
3. Strain the punch through cheesecloth. (The liquid may be cloudy.)
4. To serve, fill heatproof glasses one third full with the punch. Fill the glasses with boiling water. Garnish with cinnamon sticks, lemon twists, and cloves.

Champagne Punch

MAKES 21 CUPS

1½ cups granulated sugar
½ cup light corn syrup
2 teaspoons almond extract
Grated zest and juice of 4 lemons
⅓ cup superfine sugar
2 cups Cognac

1 cup maraschino or other cherry liqueur
1 cup dark rum
2 (750 ml) bottles cold sparkling water
2 (750 ml) bottles chilled Champagne

1. In a large deep saucepan, combine 3 cups of water with the granulated sugar and corn syrup. Bring to a boil, stirring to dissolve the sugar. Boil the liquid until a candy thermometer registers 220°F.
2. Cool the syrup to room temperature. Stir in the almond extract. Cover the syrup and store at room temperature as long as overnight.
3. To make the punch, mix the lemon zest and superfine sugar in a 2½-gallon punch bowl. Mash the zest into the sugar with a wooden spoon to bring out the lemon flavor. Pour in the lemon juice and stir to dissolve the sugar. Whisk in the sugar syrup. Stir in the Cognac, cherry liqueur, and rum. Let the mixture stand at room temperature for at least 30 minutes.
4. At serving time, slowly pour in the sparkling water and Champagne. Stir gently. Add ice.

Berrythyme Cooler

SERVES 8

Many people are eschewing alcohol these days. Let your guests know you are thinking of them by preparing a special nonalcoholic cocktail like this one.

6 tablespoons fresh thyme, or 2 tablespoons dried
2 cups boiling water
6 cups apple juice

½ cup blackberry syrup
Thyme sprigs, for garnish
Cold sparkling water, if desired

1. Place the thyme leaves in a small teapot or bowl. Pour the boiling water over them, cover, and steep for 10 minutes. Strain.
2. In a pitcher, mix the thyme tea, apple juice, and blackberry syrup. Serve the cooler over ice; garnish with a sprig of thyme. If you prefer a lighter drink, add sparkling water before serving.

HOLLINGTON HOUSE HOTEL OLD ENGLISH CIDER WASSAIL

MAKES 13 CUPS

3 cinnamon sticks

2 bay leaves

1 teaspoon whole allspice berries

1 teaspoon whole cloves

2 star anise pods

12½ cups apple cider

1¼ cups brandy

¼ cup apple brandy, such as Calvados

¼ cup honey

Whole cloves, for garnish

3 small firm eating apples, peeled, cored, and cut in 6 slices each

1. Tie the cinnamon sticks, bay leaves, allspice, cloves, and anise in a cheesecloth bag.

2. In a large pot, combine the cider, brandy, and apple brandy. Bring to a boil. Add the spice bag and the honey. Mix well. Reduce the heat and simmer gently for 10 minutes.

3. Stick several cloves in each apple slice. Add the slices to the wassail. Continue to simmer for 3 minutes longer. Discard the spice bag.

4. Serve the wassail hot or warm from a serving bowl.

MAY WINE

MAKES 16 CUPS

Dress up a punch bowl by surrounding it with a wreath ~ greens in winter, delicate blossoms in spring, and herbs in summer. This spring creation comes from one of the pioneers in herb gardening, Adelma Grenier Simmons. Hundreds of people come daily to the thirty gardens at her Caprilands in Connecticut.

5 (750 ml) bottles dry Sauternes or Moselle wine

25 sprigs sweet woodruff, plus additional for garnish

Strawberries, for garnish

Pesticide-free Johnny-jump-ups, for garnish

1. Uncork the wine. Push 5 sprigs of sweet woodruff into each bottle of wine. Recork the wine and refrigerate for 3 days.

2. To serve, pour the wine into a 1½-gallon punch bowl. Garnish with strawberries, Johnny-jump-ups, and sweet woodruff sprigs. Add ice, if desired.

SERVING CHRISTMAS CHEER

The best advice when planning cocktails for a party is to know your audience. Two drinks per person is the average; it may be plenty in some crowds, woefully short in others. With recipes for punches and cordials, be sure to consider what other beverages you'll have on hand. If cocktails are to be followed by dinner, plan on a glass or two of wine for each guest.

ROSE PETAL LIQUEUR

Turn the idea of a hostess gift upside down by presenting each of your guests with a small bottle of this very Victorian treat at the end of the evening.

3 cups loosely packed, deep pink rose petals from pesticide-free roses (about 8 large blossoms)

I quart vodka

Pinch of ground nutmeg (optional)

¼ cup lightly packed rose petals from pesticide-free rose (I small blossom)

I cup sugar

I tablespoon rose water (optional)

Red food coloring (optional)

1. Remove the white heels from 3 cups of rose petals. Gently wash the petals in cool water and dry them. Crush them lightly.

2. In 1½-quart glass or enamel container, combine the rose petals, vodka, and nutmeg. Cover. Let the mixture stand in a cool, dark place to steep for 2 weeks.

3. Remove the white heels from ¼ cup of rose petals. Gently wash the petals in cool water and dry them.

4. Layer the sugar and rose petals in an airtight pint container. Cover and let stand for I week.

5. Remove the petals from the sugar. The sugar will be lumpy.

6. In a small saucepan, gently boil the rose petal sugar and ½ cup water over medium heat for 3 minutes, stirring often to dissolve the sugar. Cool the sugar water, cover it, and refrigerate the syrup until you are ready to use it.

7. When the mixture has steeped for 2 weeks, strain it through a coffee filter into a clean glass container.

8. Stir in the sugar syrup to taste.

9. For a more pronounced rose flavor, add the rose water. If desired, stir in a few drops of red food coloring to make a deep pink color.

10. Serve the liqueur cold, after dinner, or mix it with Champagne or sparkling water.

What could be prettier than a bottle covered with an icy flower jacket? To make one, fill a milk carton halfway with water. Add flowers or herbs and a bottle containing vodka or aquavit and freeze. Then fill to the top with water and flowers. Freeze again. Remove the carton and place the bottle on your table, in a bowl to hold the drips.

TENDER VIOLETS

It takes some effort to coax Violet Kir from the tender petals, but the reward is a refreshing drink full of color that is both dramatic and sentimental. Be sure to use fresh lemon juice; the taste is superior to bottled juice. The Violet Syrup can also substitute for raspberry puree in Mascarpone Coeur à la Crème on page 174.

VIOLET KIR

SERVES 6

For this delicate cocktail, distilled water must be used to make the violet infusion. The chemicals in tap water vary from community to community and can alter the color of the infusion. When steeping, take care not to bruise the blossoms, or the infusion may become cloudy.

VIOLET INFUSION
1 cup very lightly packed pesticide-free violet blossoms without stems

1 cup plus 2 tablespoons distilled water

VIOLET SYRUP
Strained juice from 1 lemon

1 cup Violet Infusion

2 cups sugar

VIOLET KIR
6 tablespoons Violet Syrup

1 (750 ml) bottle Champagne or sparkling water

Pesticide-free violets, pansies, or Johnny-jump-ups, for garnish

1. To make the violet infusion, place the violet blossoms in a pint jar. In a nonreactive saucepan, bring the water to a boil. Pour the water into the jar, cover, and let the blossoms steep for 24 hours, turning or gently shaking the jar.
2. Strain the infusion through a sieve lined with damp cheesecloth. Discard the blossoms. Do not press the liquid out of the blossoms. The infusion will be the color of diluted blue ink in natural light.
3. To make the violet syrup, add the lemon juice, ½ teaspoon at a time, to the violet infusion while stirring until the desired color is reached. Adding the lemon juice will turn the original inky-blue color of the infusion to magenta.
4. In a medium-size saucepan, bring the infusion and sugar to a boil, stirring to dissolve the sugar. Skim off the foam and boil hard for 10 minutes. (The syrup will seem thin.) Skim off the foam again.
5. Pour the syrup into a sterilized pint bottle or jar and cap or seal it. Store in the refrigerator for up to a few days.
6. To make the violet kir, pour 1 tablespoon violet syrup into each of six Champagne flutes. Pour the Champagne or sparkling water gently down the sides of the glasses. Do not stir.
7. Garnish each glass with a violet, pansy, or Johnny-jump-up.

The Cook's Pantry

Although the notion may seem strange today, many Victorian homemakers measured their self-esteem ~ at least in part ~ through their pantries. In some households, the pantry was an entire room; in others, just a closet. It might hold pots and pans and gadgets; glass jars full of staples such as tapioca, barley, and baking powder; and bins of flour or cornmeal. Even today a well-stocked pantry can make life ~ and impromptu parties ~ easier.

Lemon Butter

MAKES 1/2 CUP

Bread and butter may seem the most pedestrian of foods, but this marriage of tastes belongs on the finest tables. For centuries, chefs have crowned their creations with butter blended with herbs. Mint is a classic partner for toast. Balls of lemon butter in a silver dish brighten any morning, and plain sweet butter, perhaps pressed into a heart mold and decorated with a few blossoms, calls to mind an old-fashioned treat. Butter flavored with maple or fruit complements pancakes or waffles.

½ cup (1 stick) unsalted butter, softened and cut up
1 tablespoon confectioners' sugar
1 teaspoon grated lemon zest
1 tablespoon lemon juice

1. In the bowl of a food processor, combine the butter, confectioners' sugar, lemon zest, and lemon juice. Process until the mixture is blended.
2. Wrap the butter in plastic wrap and refrigerate for 1 to 2 hours, until firm. Roll the butter by teaspoons into balls using butter paddles, or spoon the butter into a mold or serving dish before chilling. Well-wrapped butter will keep in the refrigerator for 1 week and in the freezer for 1 month.

Maple Pecan Butter

MAKES 2/3 CUP

½ cup toasted pecans
½ cup (I stick) unsalted butter
2 tablespoons maple syrup

I. In the bowl of a food processor, pulse the pecans with on/off turns until they are finely chopped. Remove the pecans.
2. Put the butter and maple syrup in the processor. Process until blended. Add the pecans. Process with on/off turns just until mixed.

3. Roll the butter into a log shape on plastic wrap, using the wrap to help form the log.
4. Wrap and refrigerate at least I hour before serving in slices. The butter will keep in the refrigerator for 2 weeks and in the freezer for I month.

Mint Butter

MAKES 1/2 CUP

¼ cup lightly packed mint leaves
½ cup (I stick) unsalted butter, softened and cut up
2 teaspoons mint syrup (available at specialty food shops)

I. In the bowl of a food processor, pulse the mint leaves with on/off turns until they are finely chopped. Add the butter and mint syrup. Process until blended.

Spoon the mixture into a mold or serving dish.
2. Cover and refrigerate for I hour. The butter keeps in the refrigerator for 4 or 5 days.

Honey Butter

MAKES 1 CUP

½ cup (I stick) unsalted butter, softened
½ cup honey
2 tablespoons heavy cream

I. In the small bowl of an electric mixer, beat the butter at medium speed until it is very soft. Beat in the honey until it is blended.

Gradually beat in the cream.
2. Cover and refrigerate the butter. Let it stand at room temperature to soften before serving.

STAFF OF LIFE

Presentation can make anything you serve more gracious. Bread, wrapped in fine linens or placed on an unusual cutting board, takes on a new allure.

APRICOT BUTTER

MAKES 3/4 CUP

1 cup boiling water
⅓ cup dried apricots
½ cup (1 stick) unsalted butter, softened and cut up

1. In a small bowl, pour the water over the apricots. Let them stand for 10 minutes, then drain.
2. In the bowl of a food processor, pulse the apricots with on/off turns until finely chopped. Add the butter and process until blended.
3. Line a 9-inch plate with plastic wrap. Spread the butter evenly on it, ⅛ inch thick. Cover and refrigerate for 1 to 2 hours, until very firm.
4. Cut the butter into decorative shapes using aspic cutters or small cookie cutters. The butter will keep in the refrigerator for 2 weeks and in the freezer for 1 month.

CRÈME FRAÎCHE

MAKES 2 1/2 CUPS

An American version of crème fraîche is easily made at home. In France, this smooth, tangy cream is used in sweet and savory dishes. Unlike yogurt, it won't curdle if boiled.

2 cups heavy cream, at room temperature
½ cup sour cream, at room temperature

1. In a large bowl, whisk together the heavy cream and sour cream. (Both must be at room temperature.)
2. Cover the mixture with plastic wrap and let it stand in a warm, draft-free place for 12 hours or overnight. (A gas stove with a pilot light on is ideal.)
3. Refrigerate the crème fraîche until it is cold before using it. Store it in covered containers in the refrigerator for up to 2 weeks.

VANILLA BRANDY

MAKES 1 CUP

1 cup brandy
1 vanilla bean, split in half lengthwise

Pour the brandy into a 1-pint glass jar with a tight-fitting lid. Add the vanilla bean. Seal the jar and store it at least 1 week in a cool, dark, dry place.

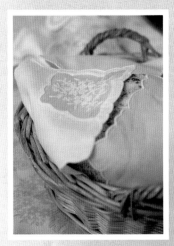

CHARLOTTE'S PIECRUST

MAKES PASTRY FOR A
9-INCH DOUBLE-CRUST PIE

Charlotte Béro gets up at one o'clock in the morning to start baking for her son's homey, cozy New York City restaurant, Anglers & Writers. She bakes from memory and taste rather than from books, and the result is that her pies are gobbled up daily. Having all the ingredients cold will improve the finished product. If you are baking the crust before filling it ~ called baking "blind" ~ prick it all over the bottom and sides with a fork, then cover it with foil and fill it with pie weights or dried beans before baking.

I tablespoon white cider vinegar
I egg
2 cups all-purpose flour
½ teaspoon baking powder

½ teaspoon salt
½ cup shortening
½ cup unsalted butter, cut in small pieces

1. In a small bowl, whisk together 5 tablespoons of ice water, the vinegar, and the egg. Reserve.

2. In a medium-size bowl, combine the flour, baking powder, and salt. Mix well. With a pastry blender or two knives, cut in the shortening and the butter until the mixture resembles coarse meal.

3. Sprinkle the flour mixture with the liquid mixture, I tablespoon at time, tossing the flour mixture with a fork after each addition until it is all moistened and the dough cleans the side of the bowl. Shape the dough into a ball.

4. Divide the dough into two-third and one-third portions, and shape each portion into a disk. Wrap each disk in plastic wrap and refrigerate for at least I hour.

5. Follow the baking directions supplied with the filling recipe. Or roll out the larger portion on a floured surface to a thickness of ¼ inch and fit it into the pie plate or tart pan. Trim the edge of the dough and crimp. Roll out the smaller portion for the top crust, or freeze for another use.

BERRY ORANGE RELISH

MAKES 1 QUART

1 large seedless orange,
    unpeeled and cut in eighths

1 (12-ounce) package fresh or
    frozen dry-pack cranberries

¾ cup sugar

2 tablespoons orange liqueur,
    such as Grand Marnier

1 half-pint fresh raspberries, or
    6 ounces frozen dry-pack
    raspberries, thawed

1. In the bowl of a food processor, pulse the orange wedges with on/off turns until they are finely chopped but not pureed. Pour the orange into a medium-size bowl.

2. In the bowl of a food processor, pulse the cranberries with on/off turns until they are finely chopped but not pureed.

3. Add the cranberries to the chopped orange. Stir in the sugar and liqueur. Fold in the raspberries. Cover the relish and refrigerate overnight.

CRANBERRY-GINGER CHUTNEY

MAKES 1 QUART

The English brought chutney back from India in the seventeenth century, and the union of sweet and savory has never left the British table. Chutneys are among the easiest preserves to make, and the most versatile: They can fill an omelet, accompany roasts, and improve a whole host of sandwiches.

⅔ cup sugar

½ cup cider vinegar

1 large seedless orange,
    chopped, including peel

½ teaspoon mustard seed

1 (12-ounce) package fresh
    cranberries

¼ cup crystallized ginger,
    finely chopped

½ cup unsalted natural
    pistachio nuts, lightly
    toasted and coarsely
    chopped

1. In a medium-size saucepan, combine the sugar with 1 cup water and the vinegar. Bring to a boil, stirring to dissolve the sugar. Add the orange and mustard seed. Simmer for 15 minutes.

2. Add the cranberries and ginger. Simmer for 10 to 15 minutes, stirring occasionally, until the berry skins pop and the mixture thickens. Remove the pan from the heat and stir in the nuts.

3. Ladle the chutney into a 1-quart storage container. Cool it on a rack. Cover the chutney and refrigerate it for up to 3 weeks.

189

PICKLED CONDIMENTS

"Next to eating such quantities of cake and pastry, I think Americans are most absurd in their free use of pickles and condiments," wrote Emma Ewing in *"Cooking and Castle Building"* in 1880. Indeed, they served pickled fruits and vegetables with many meals, using silver and crystal castors. It was the way they could taste the earth's bounty year-round, especially before homes had refrigerators.

GINGERED CARROTS

MAKES 4 PINTS

3 pounds carrots, peeled
1¾ cups sugar
¼ cup minced gingerroot

1 teaspoon pickling salt
1¾ cups white vinegar

1. Cut the carrots into sticks ¼ to ½ inch thick. Trim the sticks so that they will fit in four 1-pint canning jars, leaving a ½-inch headspace.
2. Steam the carrot sticks in a large steamer for 4 to 8 minutes, until tender-crisp. Immediately plunge them into ice water. Drain well.
3. Stand the carrot sticks in the jars.
4. In a medium-size nonreactive saucepan, combine the sugar, gingerroot, salt, vinegar, and 1¾ cups of water. Bring the mixture to a boil, stirring to dissolve the sugar. Pour it over the carrot sticks in the jars, leaving a ½-inch headspace. Adjust the lids.
5. Process the jars in a boiling-water bath (see page 11) for 10 minutes, then cool.

BREAD & BUTTER PICKLES

MAKES 4 PINTS

3 pounds firm unwaxed cucumbers
1 medium-size onion, sliced
1 garlic clove, crushed
3 tablespoons pickling salt
2 quarts ice cubes

2¼ cups sugar
1 tablespoon mustard seed
1 teaspoon celery seed
½ teaspoon ground turmeric
1½ cups white vinegar

1. Scrub the cucumbers. Cut off the ends. Cut the cucumbers in slices ¼ inch thick.
2. In a very large bowl or nonreactive pot, gently mix the cucumber slices, onion slices, and garlic. Sprinkle them with salt. Add half the ice cubes and toss to mix. Cover the top with the remaining ice cubes.
3. Cover the bowl loosely. Refrigerate for several hours.
4. Drain the vegetables, removing any unmelted ice. Discard the garlic.
5. In a large nonreactive pot, com-bine the sugar, mustard seed, celery seed, turmeric, and vinegar. Bring the mixture to a boil.
6. Add the cucumber and onion slices. Bring almost to a boil. Reduce the heat and simmer for 10 minutes, stirring often.
7. Pack the cucumber and onion slices in hot pint jars, leaving a ½-inch headspace. Ladle the cooking liquid into the jars, leaving the same headspace. Adjust the lids.
8. Process the jars in a boiling-water bath (see page 11) for 10 minutes, then cool them on a rack.

All-Purpose Vinaigrette

MAKES 3/4 CUP

2 tablespoons wine, preferably Cabernet Sauvignon or Chenin Blanc

2 tablespoons vinegar

1 tablespoon Dijon mustard

½ cup olive oil

¼ teaspoon dried oregano

¼ teaspoon dried parsley

1 garlic clove, finely minced

1. In a small bowl, whisk together the wine, vinegar, and mustard until they are blended.

2. Slowly pour in the olive oil, whisking constantly. Whisk in the oregano, parsley, and garlic.

3. Refrigerate the vinaigrette in a tightly covered jar for up to 1 week.

Vegetable Stock

MAKES 7 CUPS

2 carrots, coarsely chopped

1 medium-size onion, coarsely chopped

1 celery stalk, thickly sliced

1 large leek, green part only, sliced

1 bay leaf

3 or 4 parsley sprigs

3 or 4 thyme sprigs

10 to 12 black peppercorns

½ teaspoon salt

1. In a large saucepan or small stockpot, combine all the ingredients. Add 2 quarts of cold water. Bring the mixture to a boil and reduce the heat.

2. Cover and simmer over low heat for 20 to 25 minutes, until the vegetables are tender.

3. Strain the stock for use in soups. Reserve the vegetables for another use, if desired.

4. Keep the stock refrigerated until ready to use, or freeze for up to 6 months.

NOTE: Strained stock may be concentrated by reducing it by as much as half, yielding an intensely flavored vegetable bouillon.

PICNICKING IN PEACE

Picnics would be perfect except for the bugs. But for many people, the mosquitoes and ants are preferable to pesticides. Herbal remedies, even if not 100 percent effective, offer a third possibility. Tied in trees near the picnic, bunches of mint will repel mosquitoes. A centerpiece that includes mint or basil will help keep flies at bay. And ants will not cross tansy or catnip.

HERBAL ACCENTS

Any good-quality commercial jelly can be turned into an herbal jelly. Cook 2 cups of jelly with ¼ cup of water in a nonreactive saucepan to melt the jelly and blend with the water. Put sprigs of herbs in hot, sterilized jam jars. Ladle the hot jelly over the herbs and seal according to the manufacturer's directions. Cool and refrigerate. Try thyme with currant jelly, tarragon with apple, or devise your own.

HERB JELLY

MAKES 4 HALF-PINTS

Scented basil, parsley, lavender, rosemary, mint, tarragon, rose geranium, fennel, lemon balm, lemon verbena ~ these are just a few of the herbs you might try to make this jelly. Use juice with the sweeter herbs, cider vinegar with pungent ones.

2½ cups distilled water
1½ cups lightly packed herb leaves, crushed or chopped
¼ cup cider vinegar, or lemon or orange juice

4½ cups sugar
1 (3-ounce) pouch liquid pectin
Food coloring (optional)
Herb sprigs, for garnish

1. Bring the water to a boil and pour it over the crushed herbs. Cover and steep for 2 minutes. Strain the infusion and measure 2 cups.
2. In a 6-quart nonreactive pot, combine the herbal infusion, vinegar, and sugar. Cook, stirring constantly, over high heat to a full boil that cannot be stirred down.
3. Stir in the pectin. While stirring, bring to a vigorous boil again. Boil it hard for 1 minute, stirring constantly.
4. Remove from the heat. Stir gently and skim off any foam. Stir in a few drops of food coloring, if desired.
5. Ladle hot jelly into hot sterilized jars, leaving a ¼-inch headspace. Add an herb sprig, if desired. Seal the jars with canning lids according to the manufacturer's directions. Cool them on a rack for 24 hours. The jelly will keep in the refrigerator for 2 months.

GOLDEN CHAMPAGNE JELLY

MAKES 4 HALF-PINTS

3 cups sugar
1 cup bottled catawba grape juice
1 cup brut Champagne

¼ teaspoon powdered citric acid (available at pharmacies)
1 (3-ounce) pouch liquid pectin

1. In a deep 4-quart saucepan, combine the sugar, grape juice, Champagne, and citric acid. Cook, stirring constantly, over high heat until the mixture comes to a full boil that cannot be stirred down.
2. Add the pectin. Again cook, stirring constantly, to a full boil that cannot be stirred down. Boil for 1 minute, stirring constantly.
3. Remove the jelly from the heat, stir gently, and skim off the foam.
4. Ladle the hot jelly into hot, sterilized half-pint jars, leaving a ¼-inch headspace. Seal the jars with canning lids according to the manufacturer's directions. Cool them on a rack for 24 hours.
5. Store in the refrigerator for up to 2 months.

CHERRY MARMALADE

MAKES 9 HALF-PINTS

2½ pounds fresh pitted tart
   red cherries, or 2½
   (16-ounce) packages frozen
   dry-pack pitted tart red
   cherries, thawed (with juice)

I large orange, thinly sliced
   and finely chopped (¾ cup)

I large lemon, thinly sliced and
   finely chopped (¾ cup)

7 cups sugar

2 (3-ounce) pouches liquid
   pectin

1. In a heavy 8-quart pot, combine the cherries, orange, lemon, and sugar. Mix well. Bring to a simmer and stir until liquid forms. Simmer the mixture gently for 10 minutes, stirring occasionally.
2. Increase the heat to high. Cook, stirring constantly, to a full boil that cannot be stirred down.
3. Add the pectin. Cook, stirring constantly, to a full boil that cannot be stirred down. Boil for I minute, stirring constantly.
4. Remove the marmalade from the heat. Stir gently, skimming off the foam, for 10 minutes.
5. Ladle the hot marmalade into hot, sterilized half-pint jars, leaving a ¼-inch headspace. Seal with canning lids according to the manufacturer's directions.
6. Process in a boiling-water bath (see page 11) for 5 minutes. Cool on a rack.
7. Let the marmalade stand undisturbed for 3 to 4 days to gel, then store it in a cool, dry, dark place.

LEMON CURD

MAKES 2 3/4 CUPS

4 eggs, plus 4 egg yolks
Grated zest from 3 lemons
¾ cup fresh lemon juice

¾ cup sugar

7 tablespoons unsalted butter,
   cut up

1. In a medium-size bowl, whisk the whole eggs and yolks.
2. In a heavy large saucepan, combine the lemon zest and lemon juice, sugar, and butter. Bring to a boil, stirring to dissolve the sugar and melt the butter.
3. Gradually whisk half the hot mixture in large spoonfuls into the eggs. Whisk that back into the remaining lemon mixture in the saucepan. Cook over medium heat, whisking constantly, until the mixture becomes extremely thick and boils. Remove it from the heat.
4. Pour the lemon curd into a bowl. Press plastic wrap directly on its surface. Cool it to room temperature, about 2 hours. Refrigerate until cold, at least 2 hours.

MARMALADE

Classic marmalades include those made from Seville oranges, or a combination of citrus fruits. But many fruits, and even vegetables, have been preserved as marmalade. The British use cherries and raspberries, while Americans have created exotic kumquat as well as pumpkin and ginger varieties.

193

HERBED LIQUEURS

Bistro diners traditionally conclude a meal with a small glass of the owner's special chilled liqueur. You can make your own elixirs by steeping herbs or fruits in an alcoholic base such as vodka.

These are wonderful as drinks, as well as toppings for puddings, fruits, and ice cream. Use glass or ceramic containers, and make sure to age and keep your liqueur in a cool, dark place. Once opened, store bottles in the refrigerator.

RASPBERRY PUREE

MAKES 2 CUPS

You'll find many uses for this simple sauce. It's delightful on waffles, ice cream, or a bowl of freshly sliced peaches. It also can be pooled beneath a slice of angel food or pound cake, or drizzled over a slice of cheesecake.

4 half-pints (6 cups) fresh raspberries, or 2 (12-ounce) packages frozen dry-pack raspberries, thawed

Confectioners' sugar
Kirsch

1. In the bowl of a food processor, blend the berries in batches, pulsing on/off several times until they are liquefied. Do not overprocess, or the seeds will be ground up and impossible to remove.
2. Press the puree through a fine sieve a little at a time until all the juice is extracted. Discard the seeds.
3. Sweeten the puree to taste with confectioners' sugar and a dash of kirsch. Cover and refrigerate for up to 1 week. Stir before using.

PINK ROSES

MAKES 2 1/2 CUPS

These flowers blossom in profusion at the Pink Rose, Julie Van de Graaf's Philadelphia sweet shop. "A pink rose always reminds me of a fairy-tale birthday cake," she says. Piping roses can be mastered with a little perseverance, and the reward for the effort will be the pleasure of your guests.

1 cup shortening
1 tablespoon unsalted butter, softened
¼ teaspoon vanilla extract

2 to 2½ cups confectioners' sugar
Green and red food coloring

1. In the small bowl of an electric mixer, beat the shortening at medium speed until it is softened. Beat in the butter and vanilla until smooth. Gradually beat in the confectioners' sugar until the mixture is stiff enough to pipe through a pastry tube.
2. Spoon about ¾ cup of frosting into a small bowl. Mix in 1 or 2 drops of green food coloring.
3. Add 1 or 2 drops of red food coloring to the remaining frosting to make it light pink.
4. Using a pastry tube, pipe pink rose petals and green leaves.

Brandied Plums

SERVES 6

This is one of the classic English compotes. It's an ideal dish to make ahead for a special meal or to put in pretty jars as hostess or holiday gifts. Attach little cards suggesting serving the brandied plums with a sprinkling of sugar or on top of scoops of vanilla ice cream.

2 cups sugar, plus additional
    for garnish
2 pounds plums

½ cup brandy
1½ teaspoons vanilla extract

1. In a large saucepan, bring the sugar and 4 cups of water to a boil, stirring to dissolve the sugar. Boil for 10 minutes.
2. Add the plums, brandy, and vanilla to the mixture. Reduce the heat, cover, and simmer for 5 to 15 minutes, until the fruit is tender. The timing will depend on the size and ripeness of the plums.
3. Remove the pan from the heat. Uncover and allow the plums to cool in the syrup.
4. To serve, spoon the plums and syrup into chilled dessert dishes and sprinkle with sugar. Refrigerated, the plums will keep for up to 1 month.

Compote of Dried Fruits with Port

SERVES 4

1 cup sugar
½ cup white port wine
Juice and grated zest of
    1 lemon

2 cups mixed dried fruits such
    as apricots, figs, prunes,
    pears, and cherries

1. In a large saucepan, combine 2½ cups of water with the sugar, port, and lemon juice and zest. Bring to a boil, stirring to dissolve the sugar. Add the dried fruit. Reduce the heat, cover, and simmer for 10 minutes, or until the fruit is tender.
2. Remove the fruit from the syrup with a slotted spoon, and put it in a heatproof bowl.
3. Bring the syrup back to a boil. Boil it gently, uncovered, until it is reduced by half. Cool slightly before pouring it over the fruit.
4. To serve, spoon warm or cool fruit and syrup into dessert dishes. Or serve over ice cream or waffles. Refrigerated, the fruit in the syrup keeps for 1 month.

FRUIT BRANDIES

Serve them in your tiniest glasses and prettiest decanters. Nearly 30 pounds of ripe pears go into just one bottle of fine pear brandy, and grappa, or grape brandy, is winning new converts all the time. Raspberries, plums, and cherries are also favored for these spirits, the best of which are handmade by small orchards in this country and Europe.

Index

Recipe Credits

DEBORAH ALLEN:
Early Plantation Sugar Snap Peas & Baby Onions, James River Wild Rice Pancakes, Timbales of Macaroni & Cheese

A. J. BATAFARANO:
Vanilla Brandy, Vanilla Cream Cake, Vanilla Hazelnut Biscotti

PHILIS BENNETT:
Apple, Cranberry & Blue Cheese Strudel, Buckwheat Crêpes with Smoked Salmon, Champagne Punch, Claret Cup, Cranberry and Grand Marnier Bombe, Crêpes with Berry Filling, Frangipane Lemon Tart, Glazed Baked Ham with Orange Madeira Sauce, Honey Butter, Honey Ice Cream, Honey Waffles, Marzipan Butter Cake, Pecan Waffles, Roast Turkey with Chestnut Sauce, Sausage Stuffing for Turkey

CHARLOTTE BÉRO:
Anglers & Writers Mixed Fruit Scones, Charlotte's Piecrust, Cherry Nut Bread

MICHELLE BERRIEDALE-JOHNSON:
Summer Pudding

ROSCOE BETSILL:
Apple Almond Tartlets, Apricot Butter, Brandied Plums, Chèvre Walnut Wafers, Compote of Dried Fruits with Port, Cranberry-Ginger Chutney, Cream of Asparagus Soup, Cream of Yellow Pepper Soup, Four-Layer Poppy Seed Torte, Iced Lemon Balm Tea, Lemon Butter, Maple Pecan Butter, Mesclun au Chèvre, Mint Butter, Onion Tart with Spinach & Pine Nuts, Vegetable Stock

TERESE BLANDING:
Ginger Scones

GLORIA BOEHNER:
Brownie Torte

FRANK BROUGH:
Beggar's Purses, Chilled Spring Vegetables

DOROTHY CALIMERIS:
Chutney Cheddar Sandwiches on Walnut Bread, Cucumber Sandwiches on Potato Chive Bread, Potato Chive Bread, Smoked Salmon Canapés, Vanilla Pistachio Nut Cake

MARK & CHRISTI CARTER:
Poached Eggs with Asiago Cheese Sauce

CAROLE CLARK & JOHN MANIKOWSKI:
Vegetable Flans

MICHAEL COLLIER:
Trio of Cheesy Parcels

KEVIN CRAFTS:
Madeleines

GARY CROUSE:
Grilled Vegetable Platter

JOE CZARNECKI:
Pennsylvania Pasta with Wild Mushrooms

JAMIE & JACK DAVIES:
Golden Champagne Jelly, Grapefruit, Raspberries & Kiwifruits in Champagne, Nectarine Tart

TERESA DOUGLAS-MITCHELL:
Cinnamon Almonds, Roast Loin of Pork with Fruit Corn Bread & Sausage Stuffing, Squash Soup

BYRON FRANKLIN:
Chocolate-Dipped Strawberries, Grilled Chicken with Watercress Sandwiches, Mushroom Strudel, Pistachio Nut Bread Twists, Texas Gold Bars

MARY & EDMUND FRY:
Butterfly Fairy Cakes, Miniature Swiss Jelly Rolls

ISABELLE & VALÉRIE GANACHAUD:
Bacon Quiche Tartlets

KEVIN GARVIN:
Herbed Scrambled Eggs, Lobster Salad with Fresh Mango

RONALD & SUSAN GIBSON:
Father Christmas Shortbread

CURTIS GRACE:
Feather-Light Biscuits with Country Ham, Petits Fours, Tea Fruit Punch

PAUL GROSZ:
Mixed-Berry Sorbet, Whole-Wheat French Bread

LAUREN GROVEMAN:
Herbed Focaccia

JOHN GUY:
Hollington House Hotel Old English Cider Wassail

CERI HADDA:
Bread & Butter Pickles, Gingered Carrots

DON HAYNIE:
Curried Carrot Soup

PATRICIA HEGARTY:
Herb Salad

AINA HENEGAR:
Barley & Wild Rice Pilaf, Salmon & Wild Mushroom Chowder

BETH HENSPERGER:
Amaretti Rhubarb Coffee Cake

JOHN HUDSPETH:
Omelet with Smoked Ham &
Cheddar Cheese

HUNSTRETE HOUSE:
Hunstrete House Punch

ETIENNE JAULIN:
Marinated Ahi Tuna Steaks, Purple Basil
Ice Cream, Roasted Maryland Crab Cakes,
Tarte Tatin

SUSAN KOCHMAN:
Berry Orange Relish, Cornbread with Fresh
Corn, Cranberry Pear Compote, Herb-
Roasted New Potatoes, Mapled Brussels
Sprouts, Mushroom-Leek Frittata, Smoked
Turkey Salad, Wild Mushroom Bisque

EDNA LEWIS:
Benne Seed Biscuits, Buttermilk Biscuits,
Flounder in Parchment with Mixed Vegetables

DONNA TABBERT LONG:
Cherry Cobler, Cherry Marmalade

JOE LUPPI:
Classic Lemonade

DIANE MARGARITIS:
Lemon Poppy Muffins, Pear Raspberry Tart

MC CHARLES HOUSE:
Peachy Summer Cooler

JOY MCCONNELL:
Flaming Plum Pudding

WILLIAM MCNAMEE:
Fruit Barquettes

PATRICK O'CONNELL:
Endive & Watercress Salad, Mascarpone
Coeur à la Crème

FRED PARKS:
Scalloped Oysters

MARLENE PARRISH:
Broiled Ginger Chicken, California Fruitcake,
Canadian White Fruitcake, Chicken Salad
with Ginger Mayonnaise, Ginger Cream
Cookie Sandwiches, Violet Kir

AARON PATTERSON:
Lemon Curd

ANNA PUMP:
Lemon Bars

FLORENCE PURNELL:
Vegetable Tart

LYNN RINGLAND:
Fruit & Nut Ring with Glaze

TRISHA ROMANCE:
Berry Trifle

JULEE ROSSO:
Sage Sausage Patties

JANET SAGHATELIAN:
Camembert with Wine & Pistachio
Nuts, Port-Cheddar Spread, Strawberry
Cream Cheese

PIERRE SAINT-DENIS:
Vegetable Terrine

VICKI SEBASTIANI:
Ricotta-Stuffed Squash Blossoms

RENEE SHEPHERD:
Confetti Rice with Two Basils, Lemon Basil
Herbed Rice, Nasturtium Shrimp Salad,
Sorrel & Nectarine Salad

ADELMA GRENIER SIMMONS:
May Wine

DOLORES SNYDER:
Stilton Cheese Spread with Sliced Pears,
Wensleydale Apple Cake

EMELIE TOLLEY:
Afternoon Tea, Beef Stew with Bouquet
Garni, Berrythyme Cooler, Chèvre Herb
Crisps, Chicken Pot Pie with Parsley Crust,
Chocolate Mint Cream, Cold Cucumber
Burnet Soup, Egg Salad with Salad Burnet &
Chive Blossoms, Green-Herb Soup, Herbed
Gougères, Herb Jelly, Lavender Ice Cream,
Lemon Cream Nasturtium Sandwiches,
Lemon Geranium Pound Cake, New Potato
Salad with Hazelnuts, Orange Clove Tea,
Rose Almond Milk, Rose Petal Liqueur, Sage
& Cheddar Cheese Melties, Strawberry
Cream Cake with Nasturtiums, Sun-Dried
Tomato & Basil Sandwiches, Tarragon
Chicken Salad with Borage Blossoms,
Tomato-Mushroom Salad, Tomato Provençal
Sandwiches, Tuna Sandwiches with Thyme
Blossoms, Zesty Pea Salad

BOB TRINCHERO:
All-Purpose Vinaigrette, Spaghetti Primavera,
Zinfandel Marinated Chicken

JULIE VAN DE GRAFF:
Chocolate Hazelnut Heart Cake, Orange
Chocolate Truffles, Peach Pie, Pink Roses

DAVID WALTUCK:
Salmon with Chanterelles

DAVID WOOD:
Almond Tuiles, Crème Fraîche,
Framboise Cheesecake, Raspberry Plum Pie,
Raspberry Puree

ANTONY WORRALL-THOMPSON:
Baked Onion Soup, Gratin Dauphinois

Photography Credits

The endpapers are a collage of the work of the photographers listed above.

Conversion Table

WEIGHTS

OUNCES & POUNDS	METRICS
¼ ounce	7 grams
⅓ ounce	10 grams
½ ounce	14 grams
1 ounce	28 grams
1¾ ounces	50 grams
2 ounces	57 grams
2⅔ ounces	75 grams
3 ounces	85 grams
3½ ounces	100 grams
4 ounces (¼ pound)	114 grams
6 ounces	170 grams
8 ounces (½ pound)	227 grams
9 ounces	250 grams
16 ounces (1 pound)	464 grams
1.1 pounds	500 grams
2.2 pounds	1,000 grams (1 kilogram)

TEMPERATURES

°F (FAHRENHEIT)	°C (CENTIGRADE OR CELSIUS)
32 (water freezes)	0
108-110 (warm)	42-43
140	60
203 (water simmers)	95
212 (water boils)	100
225 (very slow oven)	107.2
245	120
266	130
300 (slow oven)	149
350 (moderate oven)	177
375	191
400 (hot oven)	205
425	218
450	232
500 (very hot oven)	260

LIQUID MEASURES

tsp.: teaspoon
Tbs.: tablespoon
8 ounces = 1 cup

U.S. SPOONS & CUPS	METRIC EQUIVALENTS
1 tsp.	5 milliliters
2 tsp.	10 milliliters
3 tsp. (1 Tbs.)	15 milliliters
3⅓ Tbs	½ deciliter (50 milliliters)
¼ cup	60 milliliters
⅓ cup	85 milliliters

U.S. SPOONS & CUPS	METRIC EQUIVALENTS
⅓ cup + 1 Tbs.	1 deciliter (100 milliliters)
1 cup	240 milliliters
1 cup + 1¼ Tbs.	¼ liter
2 cups	480 milliliters
2 cups + 2½ Tbs.	½ liter
4 cups	960 milliliters
4⅓ cups	1 liter (1,000 milliliters)